Poem

Page Number

To

From

Reflections of Southbreeze

BY EVELYN MANN

TATE PUBLISHING, LLC

Published in the United States of America
By TATE PUBLISHING, LLC

All Scripture references are King James Version,
unless otherwise indicated.

Book Design by TATE PUBLISHING, LLC.

Printed in the United States of America by
TATE PUBLISHING, LLC
127 East Trade Center Terrace
Mustang, OK 73064
(888) 361-9473

Publisher's Cataloging in Publication

Mann, Evelyn

Reflections of Southbreeze/Evelyn Mann

Originally published in Mustang,OK:TATE PUBLISHING:2004

1. Poetry 2. Spiritual 3. Family

ISBN 0-9752572-5-0 $13.95

First Printing: June 2004

For my Children

Robyn
Bonnie
Cindy
David

Acknowledgement

Each and every poem in this book has been written from my heart. Many have been prayed over, asking our Father to give me the words. I know that He has given me the gift of writing and I have strived to let my love for Him show in all I write. Any praise and glory that is received, I lay it at His feet for without Him, I could not have written this book. I have prayed that it will be used for His service, in giving inspiration and encouragement to all that read it. My greatest desire in life has been to serve Him. Just in the last few years, did God open the door of writing to me. Even as a young girl I had many desires of the heart and writing was one of them as depicted in the poem that follows. I pray that it will give hope to many, and acknowledge that the *desires of the heart* are known by our Heavenly Father and he granted me my wish to become a writer!

My Heart's Desire

I think of all my heart desires,
And the things I have missed.
Looking back when just a young girl,
I remember things I wished.

I would wish upon a rainbow,
After unexpected rain.
Wished upon a star as it,
Fell from its domain.

I wished I could be an artist,
Paint sunsets and flowers.
Beautiful buds that would open,
After springtime showers.

I wished to go to a distant land,
See all there was to see.
Throw coins into a fountain as,
I made a wish for me.

I wished to be a writer and,
A Book of poems to write.
To write of things that I love and,
The things that are in sight.

Sleeping Beauty I wished to be,
With a kiss to awake.
Live forever after with a Prince,
And his bride he would make.

Oh, the things that I did wish for!
They're still a part of me.
Especially when I am surrounded,
With beautiful things I see.

- Evelyn Mann

Table of Contents

11

Evelyn Mann

Friendship

Evelyn Mann

A Friend Like You

Oh what a wondrous thing it is,
To have a friend like you.
Whenever I'm lonely or feeling sad,
You know just what to do.

You lift me to our Father above,
With a prayer that's so sincere.
I can feel His hand upon me,
Without a doubt I know He's near.

If you need a friend to say a prayer,
Don't forget to call on me.
I'm always ready and willing,
Because friends we'll always be.

One Sweet Smile

Anytime I feel downhearted,
Or I'm feeling kinda blue,
All I ever need to do,
Is stop and take a look at you.

You always have a ready smile,
To share with all you know,
If ever you're discouraged,
You never let it show.

It lifts me up and makes me smile,
To have a friend like you.
Because I know you really care,
By all the things you do.

My sweet friend remember this,
In whatever you say or do.
Nothing more could mean as much,
As one sweet smile from you.

Evelyn Mann

Special Someone

There is a special someone,
That's always in my heart.
Someone that's a part of me,
Even when we are apart.

I think of all the good times and,
The fun times that we shared.
All the walks and talks we had,
We knew each other cared.

I won't forget the laughter or,
The smiles we shared each day.
Whenever we were together,
We both had much to say!

We made a lot of memories,
In my heart I always knew.
That this was a special someone,
And that dear friend is you!

I Met Him In A Poem

I met him in a poem one night,
Knew right from the start.
Our Father had sent someone to me,
Who would stir my heart.

His sweet words reflect his witness,
Words so sweet and true.
Some make me smile and happy,
Just turn my skies to blue.

Yet sometimes I can shed a tear,
At thoughts his words impart.
He understands the sufferings,
Writes scriptures from his heart.

He gives me hope and courage,
With the words he does give.
He often brings remembrance,
Of the life I've yet to live.

Evelyn Mann

Just Like Mom

There is someone in my life,
Who wants the best for me.
Even though we are apart,
She helps me things to see.

Always there to understand,
Her thoughts are not judgmental.
She loves me just the way I am,
In my life is instrumental.

Because of her my life is changed,
There is no turning back.
She gives me hope and courage,
To always stay on track.

She's everything a Mom should be,
Even though she's just a friend.
With heartfelt thanks and lots of love,
These thoughts to you I send.

Crossed Paths

Our Father works in many ways,
That His plan may be complete.
He may cross our paths with someone,
In order that we may meet.

It can happen in the strangest way,
When it's least expected.
His plan begins to take its form,
In ways that's not detected.

We may find a common bond,
As friendship starts to grow.
Even find this friend is different
From any that we know.

In time we'll know the reason,
He will help us understand.
A better person we will be,
Just as our Father planned.

Baby Angel

When I see a baby sweet and soft,
My heart just skips a beat.
Especially when it smiles at me,
Whenever we do meet.

Our Father whispered words of love,
When this angel he did send.
I know this is a special child,
This child that he does lend.

He placed this baby in caring hands,
To love and guide each day.
Whatever the purpose or reason,
Only our Father can say.

A precious gift to be thankful for,
One given with lots of love.
A special baby angel sent,
With blessings from above.

Fun With Me

If I could choose a day of fun,
I know just what I'd do.
First I'd take you by the hand,
So you could have fun too!

We'd float up to the clouds so high,
Play tag and hide and seek.
Look for where a rainbow starts,
Find how the colors meet.

We could look around for angels;
They must come there and play!
We could ask them all to join us,
As we play all through the day.

We could make funny faces,
In the clouds for all to see.
Try to keep them guessing,
Which one is you or me.

If ever you want a day of fun,
And you'd like to go with me,
Just know there is no one else,
With whom I'd rather be.

Friends Forevermore

You mean so much to me,
In your sweet and special way.
My love grows ever stronger,
Grows sweeter every day.

You fill my days with gladness,
In ways you know not of.
Just thinking of you inspires me,
Creates a higher resolve.

It's friends like you I feel,
That makes all others strive,
To do their best in every way,
To be glad we're alive!

I'm so thankful to have found you,
My dear sweet special friend.
Friends we'll be forevermore,
My love will never end.

Tomorrow

Tomorrow has now come again,
It has become another day.
What I'm feeling in my heart,
Is love more than yesterday.

That's the way it goes it seems,
For each day that passes by.
My love for you grows even more,
Love my heart will not deny.

I can't imagine another day,
Without you in my tomorrow.
If time you could not spend with me,
My heart would ache with sorrow.

The love we share I cherish,
Means more to me each day.
If tomorrow never comes again,
Remember these words I say . . .
I love you.

Evelyn Mann

Our Father's Angels

Our Father sends special angels,
To watch over you and me.
They are with us every day though,
Their presence we can't see.

We trust our children to their care,
When they go out to play.
Trust them to watch and protect them,
And guide them through the day.

At times my angel, I do sense,
Have things I want to say.
Most often I thank our Father for,
The angel sent my way.

Our Father has many angels;
I know they visit you too!
You'll know when they are present as,
They'll be watching over you!

All I Need

In all this world there is no one,
With whom I'd rather be.
There's none quite as beautiful,
As the one each day I see.

I love to hear your laughter,
See a smile upon your face.
When you take and hold my hand,
It's like a sweet embrace.

I don't need far away places,
Or to gaze upon a King . . .
As long as I may sit with you,
Out on the old porch swing.

So know that all I really want,
Is to have you by my side.
All the things that I may need,
You truly do provide.

Evelyn Mann

With His Love

God gave me a beautiful gift,
When He gave me a friend.
He knew just what I needed,
And knew just who to send.

I'm so glad that He did choose,
To send someone like you!
You always brightened up my day,
With all the things you do.

You are a special someone,
God uses you each day.
To let others know of His love,
As we go along our way.

I pray our Father's blessings,
Will be showered from above.
I know that He did send you,
To me with all His love.

In The Park

We walked together holding hands,
As we walked in the park today.
I couldn't seem to find any words,
Though much I wanted to say.

I knew you sensed my feelings inside,
I was aware of your beautiful love.
I felt the friendship that we share,
That was given by our Father above.

After a while we came to a path,
That led through the woods to a stream.
While there you whispered "I love you,"
I felt blessed though just a dream.

And if this dream never comes true,
I had a day in the park with you.
I heard the words I'd longed to hear,
Will remember each day this dream anew.

Evelyn Mann

My Love Forever

I know there is someone out there,
He's been waiting for me.
On the day this dream will come true,
Oh, how happy I'll be.

I've waited for him all my life;
I hope it's not too late.
I've saved my love especially,
If we should meet through fate.

I pray that he may find me soon,
So my love I may share.
I will keep dreaming of that day,
When someone for me will care.

Until he comes I'll be waiting,
I'll save my love so true.
Because it will last forever,
Forever he'll love me too.

I Set You Free

You came to me one lonely night,
When despair filled my heart.
As beautiful words embraced me,
I loved you from the start.

Wish that I had words to tell you,
What your friendship meant to me.
Each day started with a meaning,
Of sweet things that were to be.

Joy you brought that I'd not known,
With sweet and thoughtful ways.
My heart was filled with gladness,
For long and many days.

Now I know that it is time,
That I must set you free.
To search and find another,
And make happy such as me.

Evelyn Mann

As your freedom does take wing,
I pray to our Father above.
To shower you with blessings,
And an abundance of His love.
Fly safe my love . . .

Seasons Of Our Lives

Sometimes I feel so lonely, and
I want you by my side.
I think of seasons now gone past,
And all the nights I cried.

I wish things had been different,
That together we could stay.
To feel your love and sweetness, if
Just for a single day.

How I miss the fun we had:
The days of childlike play.
Together days of solitude,
When hardly a word we'd say.

I think of all the love we shared,
The days love saw us through;
Of all the things we dreamed about,
Most of which came true.

Those are the times I remember,
I'll keep them close to my heart.
I hope that you can feel my love,
   Even though we are apart.

I've learned to smile once again;
   I'm going to be okay.
The memories that I have of you,
   Will see me through each day.

Treasured Friend

There are those within my life,
That mean so much to me.
The friendship that is offered,
Is special I can see.

Some friends give me hope,
For what tomorrow brings.
They talk about our Father,
Praises to Him they sing.

There are those that I call upon,
As I journey through the day.
To help me with decisions,
And ask for them to pray.

Some friends know when I am sad,
And do their very best.
To cheer me up and make me smile,
They will not let me rest!

Of these friends that share their love,
And those I treasure too.
The one that's in my thoughts today,
My dear friend is you!

Evelyn Mann

Falling In love

Everyday I fall in love,
With you all over again.
Each day there's something new,
As the first when love began.

Words from you that seem to come,
Always unexpectedly.
Those words to you so natural,
But mean the world to me.

Smiles you bring, and laughter too,
Is like music to my ears.
A medley of love and promises,
So sweet it can bring tears.

How I thank my Lord above,
For someone as sweet as you,
And for the special love I feel,
As each day begins anew.

A Place In My Heart

I have a friend that's always there,
Ready to lend a hand.
One who cares about my heartaches,
And seems to understand.

A good friend that I can count on,
When days are so weary.
Someone to share my deepest thoughts,
When nights are so dreary.

It seems I never find the words,
To show appreciation.
The sweet friendship that is offered,
Is an inspiration.

With these true words I send my love,
And thanks I do impart.
As you my friend will always have,
A place within my heart.

A Special Love

Your love is one that's always there,
And much I'd like to say.
You fill my heart with happiness,
As dawn breaks through the day.

You understand my every thought,
And sense when days are sad.
Have always been the dearest friend,
That I have ever had.

The bond we share just seems to grow,
Your love is so sincere.
I see the love within in your eyes,
And feel it when you're near.

Together we will always be,
I know it in my heart.
Without a doubt a special love,
From which I'll never part.

Thoughts Of You

My thoughts are all of you tonight,
I know not where you are.
But my love will bring you near,
And you won't seem so far.

I wonder if you think of me,
And feel my aching heart.
The days seem to be so long,
Whenever we're apart.

I miss your smile and laughter,
The love that you do show.
That special something about you,
Just makes me love you so.

I hope that you will soon return,
In my heart remove the pain.
Of not knowing where you are,
And hold me once again.

Evelyn Mann

The Caregiver

They always try so very hard,
To give the best they can,
Caring for those that they do love,
That are so much in demand.

They show concern with thoughtful ways,
Though days may seem so long.
Keep their patience and their tongue,
When their patient is headstrong!

Some nights they may not sleep at all,
So weary they may be.
They ask our Lord for strength and help,
When they fall upon their knee.

These are the ones that most deserve,
The best that life can bring.
They do their best to add a touch,
Of love to everything.

Across The Miles

As I remember my dear friend,
What you have meant to me.
I know that I've been truly blessed,
In ways you cannot see.

I look forward to each day as,
You reach across the miles.
The friendship shared throughout the day,
Does linger all the while.

From different worlds we two may be,
And yet we're much the same.
Our love for God creates a bond,
As we praise His holy name.

Thank you for the friendship you give,
To all that need a friend.
For encouragement and support,
And the shoulder you lend.

Face to face we will meet someday,
And as I take your hand,
I'll still be giving thanks to God,
That beside you I do stand.

Evelyn Mann

Cyber Sister

Although we two have never met,
You have become so dear.
The words you write to me each day,
Brings you so very near.

To me you are more like family,
Than just an online friend.
You're now my Cyber Sister! And,
I love the time we spend.

Together we find time to laugh,
And make each other smile.
It's good to know that someone cares,
If only for a while.

On the days I'm feeling blue and sad,
A shoulder you do lend.
You do your best to cheer me up,
With happy thoughts you send.

May our Father bless our friendship,
And I thank Him every day.
For YOU my Cyber Sister!
As each day to Him I pray.

My God Child

Precious God Child I'm so thankful,
In your life to have a part.
I knew I would truly love you,
And you would bless my heart.

I promise always to do my best,
To never disappoint you.
To be there when you need me and,
Be a part of things you do.

I hope to fill your life with cheer;
Hope to give a goodnight kiss.
I know that when we are apart,
Oh precious one I'll miss!

I look forward to sweet memories,
As together time we spend.
Endless fun, long walks and talks,
And pray they'll never end!

Evelyn Mann

Precious Friends

There is nothing that's more precious,
Than friends God sends to me.
The friendship offered every day,
Is just a joy to see.

Always there to lend support,
Whenever things go wrong.
They know when I feel sad and blue,
Won't let me stay there long!

Many faults I know I have,
But they don't seem to mind.
They are kind to overlook them,
Better friends I could not find.

I thank my Father for my friends,
Whose colors are true blue.
Who journey with me all the day,
Are there to help me through.

And so these words I say to you,
In hopes they will convey.
The love I feel for you my friend,
That's in my heart today.

Loving Touch

It's the ending of the day and,
I am thinking of you.
Thinking of how much I love you,
And how I miss you too.

I think of your beautiful smile,
Your eyes that say so much.
Wishing that I could be with you,
And feel your loving touch.

I know I will always love you,
There's no one else for me.
The two of us together is.
Something meant to be.

It's so good to have someone lend,
A shoulder when needed;
Someone cheering on the sidelines,
When I have succeeded.

Evelyn Mann

You care about my every need,
Though we are miles apart.
Your sweetness and thoughtfulness,
Has surely won my heart.

I pray you will always love me,
Now and forevermore.
Because you are my sweetheart,
The one that I adore.

Saying Goodnight

It's hard to end the day as,
We go our separate way.
I feel a part of me is empty,
As goodnight I say.

I wonder if you feel my love;
If you're thinking of me.
I'll look forward to tomorrow,
And hope with you to be.

Such precious memories you give,
With your sweet and thoughtful way.
You know the things that make me smile,
Always sweet words to say.

I hope you know that I love you,
With you I want to be.
You are my dearest sweetheart and,
You mean so much to me.

Until tomorrow when the day will break
I'll hold your love so tight,
Hoping to have dreams of you and,
Wishing you sweet Goodnight.

Moonlight

Moonlight casts a magical spell,
When It falls on the one I love.
It makes me stop and thank the One,
Who sends it from above.

Somehow the night seems different,
You don't seem far away.
I see moonbeams shining down and,
There's much I want to say.

I know you see the same moon too,
That you think of me.
Underneath those magic moonbeams,
With me you want to be.

Just know whenever the moon you see,
You are within my heart.
The magic will live on my love,
From you I'll never part.

Seasons Of My Love

I waited for you in the Springtime,
You were always in my dreams.
Sometimes I could feel you so near,
Could feel your love it seems.

I looked for you in the Summertime,
So sure that you'd be there.
With the ending of the season,
Couldn't find you anywhere.

Now in the Autumn of my life,
I have found you at last.
Gone are the days of waiting and,
These seasons have now passed.

I now look forward to Winter,
Because you're by my side.
I'm thankful each and every day,
For love that never died.

Evelyn Mann

Cherished Friend

What a cherished friend you are!
To me you mean so much.
So many things you care about,
And give a needed touch.

You're there to see me through,
The hardest of my days.
Always lending a helping hand,
With sweet and thoughtful ways.

You fill my days with so much joy,
By all the things you do.
I thank our Father for giving me,
A cherished friend like you.

You make the world a nicer place,
For everyone you touch.
That's why your are loved in return,
By others oh so much!

Music

Music can bring back memories,
That sometimes we forget.
We may hear a song and remember,
Someone that we once met.

Sometimes I think of my Mama,
When songs of prayer I hear.
I remember her down on her knees,
Whispering prayers so dear.

Some bring us closer to our God,
Bible verses come to mind.
Scenes of Christ dying on the cross,
A sweet hymn will remind.

A long lost love is remembered,
With an old sweet love song.
The music seems to bring them near,
Although it's been so long.

Evelyn Mann

Music is a gift from God and,
Also instrumentalists that play.
They can put joy into your heart,
And brighten up your day.

I especially love a guitar,
Playing hymns from long ago.
Notes seem to flow into my heart,
Of songs I love and know.

I thank our Father up above,
For how he calls to me.
With beautiful music and words,
So His love I may see.

The Red Barn

Come on down to the old Red Barn,
There's something going on!
Country, Gospel and sort of Jazz,
Being played like I've not known!

Guys all wearing their wide brimmed hats;
Girls wearing skirts that flow.
Out on the dance floor couples are,
All making quite a show!

Those on the sidelines can't be still;
Sit there tapping their toes.
Looking for a dancing partner;
Anticipation shows.

Banjos strummed and guitars pickin',
Music plays through the rafters.
Everyone is having a great ole time,
You can tell by the laughter.

Evelyn Mann

Just grab a partner and let go,
Two steps up and to the side,
Just keep going and keep in step,
Across the floor you'll glide.

The red barn is rocking tonight,
You've got to come and see!
All the stomping and clapping hands;
It's the grandest place to be!

I'll Always Remember

I'll always remember these days,
Of having you near to me.
The days of fun and laughter,
And all those yet to be.

There's no way that you could know,
Or ways that you could see.
The special person you've become,
And what you mean to me.

Through days of bright and stormy weather,
I felt I was alone.
And yet there was a presence,
With sweetness I'd not known.

God stooped down and touched my heart,
The day that we two met.
He knew my heart would know you and,
You I'd not forget.

Evelyn Mann

God's perfect timing brought us close,
He knew I had a need.
I'll be eternally grateful for,
The one that He did lead.

Always in wonder how God plans,
And how he answers prayer.
Without Him I would have never known,
You were always there.

Sweet memories are kept within my heart,
As our Father knew I would.
That unknown presence that I felt,
Is now understood.

Auto Diagnosis

A grinding here, a shudder there,
Were things I heard and felt.
My auto had reached a crisis,
In which I had not dealt!

I headed to the auto shop,
Didn't know what to expect!
I would have to trust a mechanic,
To make a thorough check.

It was like a family member,
Was sick and needed care.
I was worried, tense and anxious,
As I waited there.

I was told a "diagnosis,"
Would be made right away!
I could wait or leave and afterward,
With check or card could pay.

Evelyn Mann

While waiting heard lots of stories,
As people came and went.
I tried not to notice when,
Their anger they would vent!

Some were biting nails and,
Made conversation light.
As they waited for their verdict,
They held their checkbook tight!

Auto problems we did share,
As we waited there together.
Wanted to take a little nap,
When subject changed to weather.

Old newspaper and nothing to do,
Took out paper and pen.
Thought I'd share this time with you, but
Unsure how it would end.

Finally my problems were fixed,
And I breathed a deep sigh.
Until I saw the bill in hand,
Which made me want to cry!

On the road again heading home,
No more shudder or grind.
I was feeling safe once again,
And lunch was on my mind!

I thought of the nice mechanic;
How he smiled and waved goodbye.
Most likely would have bought my lunch,
If I hadn't been so shy!

I'm so glad that I made a friend,
Who is a great mechanic!
Cause now when auto problems rise,
I won't have to panic!

Evelyn Mann

Going Out

There's something that's been going on,
That I've just learned about.
Something for those too young to date,
And it's called "Going Out"!

You most certainly may wonder,
When this you hear them say.
May ask them, "Where are you going?"
I'll tell you if I may!

They are not going anywhere!
It's just a phrase they use.
They don't say they have a sweetheart;
"Going Out" is what they choose!

This is a very special time,
And this they will declare.
So everyone around will know,
The fondness they both share.
Oh my!

Don't Give Up On Your Dreams

Don't ever give up on your dreams,
Or let them drown in doubt.
Remember sometimes it's the challenge,
That it's all about.

Make a pathway to your dreams,
One that's straight and true.
Keep those dreams within your heart,
And hold them close to you.

Put forth your very best efforts,
And ask God for direction.
Have no doubt that if you go wrong,
God will provide correction.

To dream is such a wonderful thing;
Thoughts of what we'd like to be.
Dreams give hope to pursue and find,
The wonderful visions we see.

Evelyn Mann

We have but one lifetime here on earth,
I want to make mine count!
Have something worthy to offer my Lord,
When I give an account.

Oh! So many visions and dreams,
That we want to come true.
A desire to be remembered,
For something we may do.

We have dreams to look forward to,
Let's not give up or forsake,
Just maybe one day we'll look back:
Know the right road we did take.

Magical Place

In my heart there is a place,
Where I love to be.
A place made up of dreams,
That only I can see.

This is a very special place,
One of magic and pretend.
Whenever I am lonely,
It is for you I send.

You may appear at anytime,
Doesn't matter how or when.
In my dreams you are there and,
The day with me you spend.

We watch the morning sun come up,
And walk the mountain trail.
Hand in hand throughout the day,
Where nature's beauty does prevail.

Evelyn Mann

I wish that you and I could stay,
In this place forever.
Though it is only in my dreams,
It is there we are together.

Her Heart Cries

She thought their love would never end.
Never once did she feel,
The love that was professed for her,
Wasn't ever real.

She gave her fragile heart to him,
Oh so willingly.
It opened up with all the love,
That possibly could be.

A heart so fragile yet unafraid,
Because her heart did trust.
Days were filled with happiness,
Never did she mistrust.

She felt her heart begin to break,
As she found him untrue.
Her heart hurts so with pain within,
And thoughts when love was new.

Evelyn Mann

It's hard for her to hide the tears,
From all of those around.
Her heart cries with so much pain,
Yet without a sound.

So now she has a broken heart,
But this she does not show.
She will hide the pain within her heart,
And none will ever know.

She asks Jesus to come near,
Prays for her heart to mend.
As He wraps his arms around her,
Sweet comfort He will lend.

Homecoming

When you were just a baby girl,
And I held you in my arms.
I knew that you would touch some hearts,
Someday with all your charms.

I've watched you as the years go by,
Through laughter and through tears.
You've brought so much happiness,
To your family through the years.

Now you're a special young lady;
Have won some young man's heart.
Just like I always knew you would,
From the very start.

Now we have a night that's special,
And you're on your first date.
I sure hope that your young man,
Won't keep you out too late!

It's the first of many Homecomings.
I know you're sure to go.
Always remember who you are and,
The family that loves you so.

Evelyn Mann

Waiting

There are many things that we can do,
To brighten someone's day.
Many ways are there for us,
To help along the way.

Let's all start the day with prayer;
Ask our Father above.
To show which of his children,
We could shower with our love.

It may be someone close to us,
Or someone far away.
That needs to know that someone cares,
And is thinking of them today.

Trust our Father to bring to mind,
The friend whom our thoughts to send.
He is waiting to be a part of,
The love we will extend.

I now reach out to you my friend!
You're the first on my list today.
I want to say I love you,
In a very special way.

A Baby and a Rose

Have you ever watched a baby,
When it sees a lovely rose?
As hands reach out to touch it,
What it's thinking no one knows.

In the eyes you see the wonder,
A smile upon the face.
When it sees God's creation,
One made with love and grace.

Both are beautiful miracles,
That need tender, gentle care.
Sent to us from Heaven,
For all on earth to share.

Lots of love they will need,
To help them as they grow.
All our special nurturing,
In both one day will show.

My Angel

You're my special little angel,
Even though you're far away.
You're always in my thoughts,
We talk most every day.

You always seem to understand,
Whenever I'm feeling sad.
You're just the sweetest angel,
That I could ever have.

Love we share is bound to grow,
Our love is so sincere.
You make me smile and happy,
Even though you are not near.

Together we will always be,
Not forgetting each other's love.
You're my angel sent from heaven,
A gift from My Father above.

A Different Time

If only I could be with you,
In a different time and place.
The longing would be ended,
Lonely nights I could erase.

Within my heart the love I feel,
I share with you each day.
The love you offer in return,
Reflects in words you say.

I know this time is not for us,
Though love is within my heart.
Distance and time is between us,
Many things keep us apart.

My love I send on angel's wings,
And for you I ask their care.
I'll keep you close within my heart,
And cherish the moments we share.

My Friend

I'm sending this to let you know,
I'm here to be your friend.
Count on me when troubles come,
My shoulder I will lend.

I'll also say a prayer for you,
And ask our Father above.
To send a special blessing,
That you may feel his love.

I'm thankful for your friendship,
You mean so much to me.
Your sweetness and your goodness,
Is there for all to see.

I wish the very best for you,
In whatever you may do.
Know that I will be a friend,
Who will always care for you.

Angel On My Shoulder

Here with me throughout the day,
The angel on my shoulder.
I feel the friendship and the care,
Each day I feel less older.

I'm reminded to be thankful,
For each new day in life.
There's a reason to be happy,
Even in the days of strife.

He stays with me on all my trips,
Especially to the park.
That's where I mostly talk to him,
Sometimes till almost dark.

He knows my deepest secrets,
We talk about my dream.
He always seems to understand,
And know just what I mean.

I hope this dear sweet angel,
With me will always stay.
Because I've come to care for him,
In a very special way.

Evelyn Mann

True Friend

There are some that stand apart,
From all others on this earth.
Just being in their presence,
Brings happiness and mirth.

I'm so thankful for the friend,
That God chose to send my way.
It makes me feel so grateful.
For friendship shared each day.

Your love for Jesus always shows,
Like a light that shines so bright.
Thinking always of others,
Helping to make things right.

Always there to be a friend,
With a friendship tested and true.
No one else could take your place,
And that dear friend is you.

The Perfect Dress

It's that time of year again and,
Tonight she has a date!
Homecoming has rolled around once more;
She'll be staying out quite late.

What a whirlwind week it has been,
Looking for the perfect dress.
Lots of decisions to be made,
But fun time nonetheless.

So many things that she must do.
Is running here and there.
She even must find someone,
She trusts to do her hair!

When it's time for the dance to go,
And her date is at the door.
I know she'll be poised and ready,
For the boy she does adore!

She's beautiful in her perfect dress,
With her eyes all aglow.
A night that will be remembered,
As off to the dance they go!

Evelyn Mann

Online Friends

There are friends we set apart,
That are different from the rest.
Each and every day that comes,
They give their very best.

Always cheer you when you're sad,
Do their best to make you smile.
They know when you are lonely,
With you they'll stay a while.

You see, these friends are different,
Because we've never met.
The only time we spend with them,
Is when we're on the net.

They are what a friend should be.
One who's loyal and true blue.
And this my dear sweet friend,
Happens to be you!

Babies and Puppy Dogs

I love babies and puppy dogs,
Both are just so sweet!
It makes me laugh and smile,
As I watch them when they meet.

Lots of hugs and kisses given,
It's hard to keep them apart.
Tail wagging and giggles too,
It just warms my heart.

Tugs of War and chasing too,
As the bond between them grows.
Sometimes even tears appear,
The reason no one knows.

When all tired out and play does end,
Best friends they have become.
They lie sleeping side by side,
With dreams of play to come.

Guardian Angel

If I were a Guardian Angel,
Although you could not see,
If one day I'm allowed to choose,
Yours I would like to be.

I'd travel with you throughout the day,
Know what you're dreaming of.
Would help you make your dreams come true,
And all your problems solve.

When bedtime comes I'd kneel with you,
Your earnest prayers I'd hear.
And although you could not hear me,
I'd pray for one so dear.

I'd sit beside your bed tonight,
And quietly watch you sleep.
Implant sweet dreams for you alone,
And know one day we'll meet.

First Kiss

I remember my first kiss,
How sweet it was to me.
A kiss so pure and innocent,
Under an apple tree.

A shy small girl felt her first love,
And yet my heart was sad.
For tomorrow he would be gone,
The dearest friend I had.

He said that he would think of me,
And write me every day.
He sang a song that afternoon,
As he walked away.

"I'll be with you in apple blossom time!"
He sang so sweet and clear.
"I'll be with you, to change your name to mine!"
To me a song so dear.

There are many years now gone past,
Since that day I was kissed.
Still, whenever I hear that song,
I wonder . . . was I missed?

Evelyn Mann

Broken Heart

What pain a broken heart does leave,
And disappointment too.
When one you love so very much,
You find has been untrue.

You wonder what it was you did,
Or something that you said.
How could a love professed so strong,
Away from you be led?

Remembering all the sweet words,
You felt were just for you,
It hurts so deep within your heart,
To find there's someone new.

Memories of days will haunt you,
And sadness you will feel.
A love thought to be so beautiful,
Was never really real.

Brokenhearted and so alone,
With just a memory.
Of how she gave her heart away,
And threw away the key.

Magic Wonderland

I'll meet you in my dreams my love,
Down by the clear cold stream.
It is this magic wonderland,
Of which I love to dream.

While there my troubles fade away,
Serene and peaceful there.
Surrounded by God's gifts to us,
Created with loving care.

I stand in awe of the beauty,
With you I want to share.
So dream a dream of me my love,
And I will meet you there.

Together we will feel God's love,
And have this time to share.
And when we wake we both will know,
We were in His precious care.

Someday In Time

Someday in time I will look back,
And I'll remember you.
Oh! Such sweet memories I have,
Of when our love was new.

Precious memories of when we met,
A dream that had come true.
Now the love that fills my heart is.
Love that I give to you.

I'll remember all the sweet times,
You made me laugh and smile,
The days that I was lonely and,
You stayed with me awhile.

Most of all I will remember,
Today I was with you.
You'll never know how much it meant,
To know you love me too.

I'll Never Forget

Be still my heart and don't be sad,
All things will work for good.
The sun will shine again I'm sure,
As our Father said it would.

It's just so hard to say goodbye,
To one that's been so dear.
One that's been closer than a friend,
And always so sincere.

Fate has led us separate ways,
But in my heart you'll be.
There'll never be another love,
That's meant as much to me.

I'll never forget the love you've shown,
And the love I'll keep for you.
A special bond between two friends,
One from which love grew.

Something Missing

Something was missing in my life,
Until you came along.
You brought the love and joy I need.
In my heart you put a song.

Sweet friendship from the beginning,
Then best friends we became.
I knew somehow that my life
Would never be the same.

I've learned what life is all about;
What things do really count.
I know that I can lean on you,
When troubles start to mount.

With loving arms you draw me close,
That's where I want to be.
To feel your presence and the love,
That means so much to me.

Heading Home

Heading for home down the Interstate,
And those that do await.
It's been a long and lonesome haul,
To deliver all the freight.

He's traveled this highway he knows,
A hundred times or more.
Seen all the scenery on the way,
No new things to explore.

Met lots of people along the way,
Some he'll never forget.
He has also done a few things,
That he'll always regret.

A CB radio connects with friends,
It helps to pass the time.
But it's "Roger, over and out!"
When he sees his Home State sign.

Evelyn Mann

When almost home he just can't wait,
To see those he does love.
Says a prayer of thankfulness to,
Our Father up above.

Home again with his family,
With presents all around,
He knows that when he's heading home,
It's like he's heaven bound.

I Miss You

A time so long and far away,
Such happiness I knew.
No lonely days and nights,
Because I was with you.

You filled my days with endless fun and,
To you I gave my heart.
Nights were filled with love and joy;
You said we'd never part.

I miss you since you've gone away,
I think of you each day.
Remembrance brings such sweet thoughts,
Of your sweet and loving way.

Oh, I love you so my darling,
Why did you have to leave?
Everyday I spend without you,
For you my heart does grieve.

For always and forever I'll,
Keep you in my heart.
My love for you will never cease,
While we are apart.

Evelyn Mann

In My Life

Into my life you came one day,
And it's not been the same.
I didn't know there was a need,
Until the day you came.

Each day has a different meaning,
Because of you my friend.
It's a beautiful kind of friendship,
Oh, the sweetness you lend.

You make me smile and make me laugh,
At the silliest little thing.
Time spent with you is so much fun;
Such joy you do bring.

We share so many different things;
We go from A to Z.
And places that I've not known,
Your visions help me see.

Thank you for your friendship sweet,
It means so much to me.
You give me peace and serenity,
With you I love to be!

Just Joey

The very first time that I saw him,
He was standing all alone.
Looking so small and lonesome,
No attention being shown.

There was just something about him,
That touched my heart so.
I asked someone about him but,
No one seemed to know.

I hardly took my eyes from this,
beautiful creation!
I knew that I would have to give,
My consideration.

Others were there that I could see,
And each one had a name.
All were pretty and so special,
But none were just the same.

Evelyn Mann

My visit soon was ended and,
I was about to leave.
Then once more he caught my eye,
For him I knew I'd grieve.

I was standing right beside him;
Looked down and saw his name.
To walk away without him would,
Surely be a shame.

"Just Joey" was given as his name,
If you or no one knows;
He now lives in my backyard as,
Just Joey is a rose.

Do You Know

Do you know that I love you?
You're all I've ever desired.
The life you live before me,
Is one that's so admired.

You seem to find the words that,
Give comfort and relief.
I know that they come from within,
And from your strong belief.

You're never too busy to say "hello"
Or with me to stay awhile.
Your funny ways and loving words,
Fill my heart with a smile!

Wanting to share so many things,
With me throughout the day.
Sometimes good, sometimes bad,
So much we have to say!

Evelyn Mann

Armed and ready for whatever comes,
You're ready to befriend.
When sadness or disappointment comes,
A shoulder you will lend.

I'm so glad that God crossed our paths,
That friends we'll always be.
These words I send so you will know,
Just what you mean to me.

Tomorrow Has Come

I wake to sweet remembrance,
Tomorrow is now here.
I left you in my dreams last night,
But still I feel you near.

I want to stay here in my dreams,
Because you were with me.
Together making memories,
That only I could see.

Underneath a moonlit sky,
We gazed upon a star.
So bright and beautiful it was,
And yet so very far.

I closed my eyes and made a wish,
That my love you could feel.
Wished this was not a dream and,
All I felt was real.

Evelyn Mann

"Tonight I love you oh so much,"
You whispered in the night.
"But tomorrow I will love you more,
When you wake in mornings light."

And so tomorrow has now come,
I know my wish came true.
As I lay here on my pillow,
I feel the love from you.

I know I'll always love you and,
Cherish dreams of you.
I pray in all my tomorrows,
My dreams of you come true.

The Red Rose

I see a rose in its beauty,
Soft petals all perfumed.
I feel it saying "I love you,"
From first when it does bloom.

A red rose from the one you love,
Means oh! so very much.
It's almost like a part of them,
Is reaching out to touch.

Also it can bring memories,
Of love that's in the past.
Can bring tears in remembrance of,
A love that did not last.

They were created to bring joy,
A gift from heaven above.
For us to share with those around,
Especially those we love.

Evelyn Mann

What a beautiful way to remind,
That love is felt for me.
I thank Him for the beauty that,
He made for me to see.

There could never be a doubt,
That my God is King:
Because only He could create,
The beauty that He brings.

Poets

There's nothing ordinary about a poet,
You are a different lot.
Writing sweet words to remind us,
Of some things we've forgot.

My heart is warmed each day that comes,
When I read your words.
When I see the beautiful poems,
Oh, how my heart is stirred!

God gave each of you the gift,
To put your thoughts in word.
Some write in rhyme and some in prose,
Either is preferred.

Your poems may be of anything,
Whatever you desire.
But all reflect what is inside,
And that's what I admire.

Evelyn Mann

You make me laugh and make me cry,
As feelings you do share.
Your words sometime affect me,
Like a breath of fresh air.

I consider each a special friend;
Our writings create a bond.
And through your words you touch my heart,
Of all I'm very fond!

Encouragement

Evelyn Mann

Fly Away

There's a bird that is watching,
That's waiting for me.
He's waiting and watching,
From high in a tree.

He sings his song,
From dawn's early light.
All through the day,
Till the darkness of night.

Fly away, fly away,
Come fly with me.
We'll soar toward the heavens,
How happy you'll be.

Fly away, come fly!
We'll glide with the wind.
I'll be right beside you,
My wings I will lend.

At the end of the day,
When we have returned,
A lesson in trust,
You will have learned.

Misunderstood Love

Sometimes things are said and done,
That we can't understand.
Things that cause hurt feelings,
Nothing seems to go as planned.

It's hard to feel that we are loved,
When love seems so unkind.
It's hard to find forgiveness,
When tears and hurt combine.

Hopefully we may all embrace,
Love which is misunderstood.
It often comes under disguise.
We can't see it as we should.

Love sometimes calls on extra strength,
To protect children He did send.
Trust Him to give understanding,
That broken hearts may mend.

Evelyn Mann

Choices

We don't always stop to think,
When choices we do make.
Sometimes we may take a path,
That leads to a grave mistake.

We live just for the moment,
As down that path we go.
Then when we face tomorrow,
Only sorrow we do know.

The price we pay is often large,
Our hearts fill with regret.
For choices we do make today,
Are some we can't forget.

Let's give the moment to our Lord,
When temptation comes our way.
Trust His strength and power,
To save us from dismay.

Forgiveness

Often we feel hurt and rejected,
By one we thought a friend.
It's hard not to feel angry and,
Days in silence we spend.

How can friendship go so wrong when,
There's such sweet memory?
Days filled with fun and laughter,
Are not what they ought to be.

If we're not willing to forgive,
Others for what they do.
We lose acceptance and respect,
Things important to me and you.

We will carry a heavy load and,
It soon will start to show.
We'll feel the weight upon our soul,
And need to let it go!

Evelyn Mann

God promises our reward to be great,
When we love and do good.
Said we should love our enemies,
Be forgiving as He would.

How can we ask God to forgive,
If others we can't forgive?
If we but ask He will help us,
Sweet memories we'll relive!

Inner Child

My inner child, as I hold you in my arms,
And rock you to and fro.
There's something I must tell you,
That I want you to know.

You trusted those around you,
As that you thought you should.
You tried to understand it all,
To withstand it as you could.

I know my child what you endured,
So innocent and sweet.
How fear would grip your heart,
When someone you did meet.

But our Father did sustain you,
Because He loved you so.
For all the pain and suffering,
That no one seemed to know.

Remember you were not to blame,
For what happened in the past.
Let's now dry and wipe your tears,
Because you're free at last!

Evelyn Mann

In God's Hands

Though there are some that have fear,
In this bewildering time.
Let us strengthen our faith in God,
And remember his love sublime.

God always has a purpose,
And always has a plan.
For those that love and follow Him,
Though we do not understand.

Let us put away our doubts,
In the darkness find the light.
Have hope and wait patiently,
For God to end our plight.

God is always with us,
Even though we cannot see.
Let us follow in His footsteps,
So His witness we may be.

As the eagle soars above the storm,
He knows the storm will end.
We are in our Father's hands,
Our country He will mend.

A Fragile Heart

Be careful when you speak of love,
To one with a fragile heart.
A heart that's easily shattered,
When love may depart.

Do not tell them they are special,
If it's not true at all.
Feeling they're on a pedestal,
Will hurt so when they fall.

A fragile heart has so much love,
That it wants to give.
Forgetting that it's vulnerable,
And pain it may relive.

The love that was will always be,
In its special place.
The place for special memories,
That cannot be erased.

So, if you have a shattered heart,
And pain there you feel.
Just ask our Heavenly Father,
For His love to reveal.

He has a love that you can trust,
And your heart He will mend.
He will wrap His arms around you.
Peace and comfort He will lend.

It Is Well With My Soul

He was a well known Christian man,
Lived over a hundred years ago.
Though some may not know his name,
His music they may know.

He lived a happy, prosperous life,
Four daughters he did sire.
All things were going well for him,
Until the "Chicago Fire."

Much of the business he had was lost,
And after speculation,
Decided to take his girls abroad,
To get their education.

A last minute circumstance,
Caused him not to go.
His wife would journey with the girls,
And courage they did show.

The day they sailed and said goodbye,
He promised to join them soon.
There was no way that he could know,
That disaster did loom.

Evelyn Mann

In mid-ocean two ships collided,
One was the Villa de Havre.
All that was left of the remains,
Was at the bottom of the sea.

From his wife he received a note,
"Saved, alone" is all it said.
Darkness and despair overcame him,
As these words he read.

Through clouds of darkness came a light,
It came from God above.
The bright light of God's promises,
Filled with comfort and love.

No matter what the circumstance,
Whether sorrows or peace,
God will never forsake us and,
His love will never cease.

With these true thoughts in mind he wrote,
The words to a song of old.
With heart filled with sorrow he penned,
"It Is Well With My Soul."

You Are Beautiful

Accept yourself for who you are,
And hold your head up high.
In God's eyes you are beautiful,
Like a precious lullaby.

It doesn't matter where you're from,
Or who you are in life.
God made you as He wanted you;
Even though you may feel strife.

He has a plan for one called "you"
And sent with you a gift.
So you might spread His love around,
And other's spirits lift.

Whenever you feel cast aside,
Take out your gift of love.
Let others see you care for them,
As God watches from above.

He will guide with tender mercies,
And blessings He will impart.
You will feel His loving presence,
As you hold Him to your heart.

And then you will feel beautiful!
As all eyes fall on you!
The beautiful person that you are,
Will show in all you do.

A Bend In The Road

Each day we have trials or triumphs;
Have joy or burdens to bear.
Whether days are stressful or calm,
I know God's love is there.

I won't let dark clouds surround me;
I'll find a brighter day.
I'll leave my doubts behind me as,
I journey on my way.

I know that He does lead me in,
The pathway I may take.
Because I've come to Him in prayer,
In decisions I must make.

Now there's a bend in the road but,
God's presence will remain.
He'll help me get where I belong,
And make me glad I came.

I'll be excited just to see,
What God does have in store!
Where He plans to lead me next,
As He opens up a door.

Evelyn Mann

With Open Arms

Sometimes we feel so all alone,
Nowhere for us to go.
We feel our lives are empty and,
Have nothing much to show.

When there's no hope to see ahead,
And feel so blue today.
If we will only trust in Him,
He'll surely show the way.

God's waiting there with open arms;
And hears our cries of pain.
His arms will keep you safe from harm,
Your needs He will sustain.

So take your burdens to our Lord,
As he has asked us to.
Trust him completely in your heart,
And He will see you through.

Sometimes 1 Feel So All Alone

When loneliness over takes us,
Abandoned we may feel.
May feel that we are all alone,
And tears we can't conceal.

It's time like this to remember,
That we are not alone.
We can take comfort in knowing,
God sees us from His throne.

He promises to be with us,
God's promises are true.
He said he'd never forsake us,
These words we can cling to.

He's with us through all the good times,
With us through the bad.
Is there when we are joyful and,
Whenever we are sad.

Evelyn Mann

We can lean on God's promises,
When loneliness we feel.
He will let us feel His love and strength,
And joy that is so real.

Adoption

She had to let you go dear child,
Could not find another way.
The day that you were born to her,
There was much she could not say.

Birthdays came and holidays too,
Many thoughts were brought to mind.
All the days that came between,
Brought love and tears combined.

She sought a better life for you,
That was filled with joy and peace.
Always prayed that you would be happy,
Knew her love would never cease.

After many years she found you,
And gives thanks to our Father above.
She asks you now to open your heart,
And allow her to share her love.

Evelyn Mann

Heartache

I'll never forget the love we had.
Even though you've found another.
Memories will linger in my heart,
Be remembered as no other.

I felt heartache and much grief,
All through the day and night.
Felt my world was falling apart,
No happiness was in sight.

Then one night I heard a voice,
Which whispered words of love.
I knew I could abound in hope,
Look for comfort from above.

In my Father's hands I put my trust,
In time He will open a door.
I'll find the one He sends for me,
Love will last forevermore.

Regrets

I wish that I could turn back time,
Spend one more day with you.
There are many things left undone,
That I want to say and do.

My heart is full of regrets,
For the things I did and said.
In remembrance of these things,
Many tears have been shed.

Our Father above has told us,
That forgiveness is in sight.
So I'm turning it over to Him,
To change darkness into light.

I'm going to take a different road,
Watch what I say and do.
Hope that somehow you will know,
These things I owe to you.

His Perfect Choice

When I remember back in time,
It's hard for me to know,
That things are wrong between us,
As through the days we go.

I know our Father had a plan,
When He brought us two together.
I thought our love would be sustained,
Through fair or stormy weather.

Somehow I know that we have strayed,
From the path that He did choose.
If we don't steer back toward that path,
Our love we just might lose.

I ask that you do pray with me,
And listen carefully to His voice.
God will gently restore our love,
For us, His perfect choice.

United We Stand

Our eyes were full of tears today,
As we watched them leave.
Off to a distant foreign shore,
For them our hearts will grieve.

They are husbands, sons and fathers,
All facing the unknown.
Committed to fight for freedom,
In a far away war zone.

A silent bond between those left,
As we begin to pray.
Asking God to protect them all,
Watch over them each day.

For our Service Men and Women,
Our hearts are full of pride.
We know whatever does befall,
Our God is by their side.

Evelyn Mann

We will look forward to the day,
When loved ones will return.
With them they will bring victory!
And peace for which we yearn.

Let's lift our voice to God in prayer,
Ask Him to bless our land.
Pray for those in authority,
As united we stand!

To Know For Me You Pray

What a wonderful thing it is,
To know for me you pray.
How sweet it is to know you care,
And think of me today.

I know that I am truly blessed,
To have you for a friend.
Your love for others and deep faith,
Shows in prayer you spend.

Whenever I need a friend to pray,
I know you're always there.
Someone that's understanding,
Of things I need to share

I know that I can call on you,
For me to intercede.
Thank you for unwavering love,
And being a friend in need.

Evelyn Mann

He'll Take Us Places

Sometimes when we stray from God's path,
We stumble along the way.
We can't seem to follow his footsteps,
Just wander all the day.

Life seems to whirl out of control,
Everything just goes wrong.
The path to the mountain top,
Takes oh so very long.

So in the valley we roam and,
Try paths that are unknown.
As our God watches from above,
He knows the path is wrong.

If we seek Him he'll show the way,
His presence is always near.
He'll give us comfort and strength,
And take away all fear.

He'll take us places we've not been,
What glorious things we'll see!
He'll help us reach that mountaintop,
If we fall upon our knee.

God Will Answer

We search for answers to questions,
When the outlook is not good.
Lot's of time is spent in worry,
And fret more than we should.

Small problems can become mountains;
Not knowing what to do.
Dark shadows cast over our lives;
We wish we could start anew.

We forget our future is in God's hands,
He's always in control.
He knows everything we may need,
As each day starts to unfold.

We must depend upon God's grace,
To give the answers we seek.
And if we listen carefully,
To our heart He will speak.

God is faithful in His promises,
And His word is true.
All we need to do is seek Him.
Each day He'll see us through.

Evelyn Mann

Decisions

Sometimes we are uncertain,
And decisions must be made.
It may be very complex,
and choices go unmade.

We need someone to help us,
And tell us what to do.
Know we've made right choices.
And feel secure about them too.

If we'll only follow Jesus,
We will find a clear direction.
He will light the path for us,
And give the path protection.

To His control if we but yield,
Decisions He'll help us make.
We'll feel our Father's presence,
The right directions we will take.

Burden Of Guilt

Guilty feelings we may have,
Down deep within our heart.
Year by year it seems to last,
From us it will not part.

If we but ask there is a friend,
In whom we may confide.
He's the one to calm our fear,
And free the guilt inside.

Let's place our burdens at His feet,
Have faith He will forgive.
No longer should we feel this guilt,
Or with this burden live.

Our Lord is good and merciful;
He knows what is in our heart.
His forgiveness will bring us peace,
Guilty feelings from us will part.

Family

Evelyn Mann

My Son

The day that you were born my Son,
How my joy did overflow.
As I gently held you in my arms,
Oh! how I loved you so.

I knew you were a gift from God,
That I should lead and guide the way.
Everyday I prayed to Him,
To give me words to say.

The years slipped by one by one,
I taught you right from wrong.
Our Father told me what to teach,
As adulthood came along.

Now my Son you're all grown up,
I stand back and look with pride.
At the wonderful Son that I have raised,
With our Father by my side.

Grandma

Grandma when I think of you,
My heart just fills with love.
You stand for all the things I know,
That is taught us from above.

When I succeed you're always proud,
Are among the first to tell me.
Your faith helped me achieve my goal,
To become what I want to be.

I know your love reaches out to me,
I can feel it across the miles.
I can picture that dear face of yours,
That is always full of smiles.

I'll always remember the love and care,
That you have given through the years.
How with open arms you've held me,
And kissed away my tears.

Evelyn Mann

To Comfort You My Daughter

Across the miles I send my love,
And prayers for you today.
That you'll feel our Father's presence,
Feel His love throughout the day.

So many things I'd like to say,
Wish I could kiss away each tear.
My heart is full of love for you,
For to me you are so dear.

There is no greater friend on earth,
Than the one I call my Daughter.
Now is the time that most of all,
We can comfort one another.

I hope my love gives you comfort,
Just know I'm thinking of you.
I'm with you in love and spirit,
For now and for always too!

Granddaughter

Memories that I have of you,
I keep close within my heart.
The days of fun and laughter,
From those I will not part.

I remember the sweetest days,
Those I held you in my arms.
Rocking gently as you lay,
Entranced by all your charms.

I wonder what life offers,
For one as sweet as you.
Beauty that is yours within,
Reflects in all you do.

I think about you every day,
And hope you think of me.
I pray that you may become,
All things you want to be.

Evelyn Mann

Tuck some memories in your heart,
Those that you hold dear.
And when you find one of me,
Just know that I am near.

I wish for you Granddaughter,
The best that life may give.
Our Father's love and blessings,
Upon each day you live.

My Brother

What a blessing it has been,
To have you for my Brother!
The feeling that I have for you,
Is special as none other.

Always there when I am sad,
Telling me of our Father's love.
You help me see the blessings,
He has sent me from above.

Whenever I may need a friend,
I know I can call on you.
You always know just how to help,
In the things you say and do.

There will always be a place for you,
One that I have set apart.
It's filled with love and thankfulness.
For YOU! within my heart.

Evelyn Mann

Your Wedding Day

My dear son as you come to wed,
My heart is full of pride.
Soon you give your wedding vows,
And take a lovely bride.

I wish for you the best there is,
In whatever you may do.
As together you now make a home,
And start a life brand new.

If ever you need me I'll be here,
To help in any way.
Know that you'll be in my thoughts,
Each and every day.

God bless and keep you safe,
As the years you journey through.
May the love between you,
Show forth in all you do.

You Became Our Family

Many days I waited for you,
Felt longing in my heart.
When first that I did see you,
I loved you from the start.

A precious angel from God above,
That came from loving arms.
You simply took my breath away,
With all your little charms.

Loving and sweet as time went by,
You became our family.
No dearer that a child could be,
Than what you've been to me.

Now my child I set you free,
To share your precious love.
With others that have found you,
With guidance from above.

Evelyn Mann

A Grandmother's Love

I always knew within my heart,
God sent you from above.
The glorious day you were born,
I felt our Father's love.

As I saw those tiny little hands,
Reach out to touch someone,
My heart was full of happiness,
A new life had begun!

And now our task on earth begins,
To help you as you grow.
We must teach you love and kindness;
Our Father you must know!

He put you in our loving care,
And put you in my heart.
You will always be my angel,
Together or apart.

There are many wonderful things,
That I will pray for you.
There's special love in my heart and,
I know you'll love me too.

My Sweet Sam

There's a certain little fellow,
That likes to cuddle up with me.
Wants to cuddle all the time,
He's a puppy dog you see.

Daylight starts with trips outside,
And continues through the day.
Doggy toys strewn about,
Keeps my house in disarray!

Lots of loving hugs he gets,
But gets some scolding too.
Loves to chew on everything,
Especially on my shoe!

He runs and plays through the day;
Often stops to take a nap.
At night he has just one desire;
To fall asleep upon my lap.

Since he's come into my life,
Days have a different start.
I never knew a puppy dog,
Could absolutely win my heart!

Evelyn Mann

My Daughter

My Daughter, when I think of you,
My heart's so full of love.
I know that you were sent to me,
As a gift from above.

I think of the child you once were,
And though the years go fast,
The days of sweet hugs and kisses,
Are memories that last.

The woman that you've now become,
Just fills my heart with pride.
The love and kindness that you show,
Comes from deep inside.

Everyday you make time for me,
Sweet words I hear you say.
Sometimes it's just a word or two,
As "Mom are you okay?"

Thank you for the Daughter you are,
And company you lend.
You are not only my daughter,
But also my best friend.

Single Dad

It so hard for a single Dad,
To know just what to say.
To help my children understand,
Why I am gone each day.

I come home to an empty house,
There's none to greet me there.
No sound of laughter or of play,
Or hugs that I may share.

I go for walks and wish that we,
Were together once again.
I have memories of days past,
When we were happy then.

I long to hear them call my name,
And I anticipate,
The times they're in my arms once more,
Though hard it is to wait.

When our visits come to an end,
I feel my heart will break,
And hope that each will carry home,
Sweet memories we did make.

Evelyn Mann

Grandma and Granddad

I wonder if you'll ever know,
Just what you mean to me,
And all the many joys you've brought,
To all the family.

You taught me of our Father's love,
And how He cares for me.
Together we asked for guidance,
In things we could not see.

You told me how Christ lived and died,
For all humanity.
I gave my life to Him one day,
Like Him, I've tried to be.

You've always asked for so little,
And yet, given so much.
Each day there seems to be someone,
Whose life that you have touched.

I'm sending this so you may know,
Much love I feel for you,
I know that whether near or far,
That you do love me too.

Empty Chair

This chair knows all my heartaches,
It's where I sit to pray.
It also knows my heart's desires,
As I begin each day.

It's in this chair that I recall,
Sitting on my Granddad's knee.
He told me of our Father's love;
Read the Bible to me.

He taught me to disregard when,
Unkind words I hear.
He comforted and drew me close.
And wiped away my tear.

He was a plain and simple man,
With a love for all others.
Treated all with great respect as,
God said they were his Brothers.

This old chair is dear to me,
Fond memories it does bring.
Of days I can't bring back but,
It makes my heart still sing!

Dad

Before another day goes by,
I want to say I love you.
Will remember your sweet love,
That shows in all you do.

Whenever trouble comes along,
Your helping hand is there.
With sweet and tender feelings,
Your wisdom you do share.

Through the years you had a part,
In dreams that have come true,
You give me hope and courage,
For the things that I must do.

Memories of you I'll never forget,
Or the special love we share.
That when I needed someone,
My DAD was always there.

I Await You Daughter

Of all the wonderful blessings,
That have been bestowed on me,
None could mean quite as much,
As the daughter that's yet to be.

I close my eyes and dream each day,
Of the things I'm going to say.
When first I hold you in my arms,
And against my heart you lay.

I'll tell you of your Mother's love,
Of hopes and dreams for you,
That our Father will be with you,
In whatever you may do.

I await you now my daughter dear,
With a heart so full of love,
That nothing could surpass it,
Except our Father's love above.

Evelyn Mann

Grandson

The day you came into our lives,
We were truly blessed.
You've been the perfect Grandson,
God sent the very best!

It seems like only yesterday,
You were a baby boy.
One who was loved by everyone,
And brought your family joy.

Through the years your precious smile,
Has brightened up each day.
The time that you do spend with me,
Means more than words can say.

Much happiness I wish for you,
In all the years to come.
Remember always, I love you.
I'm so proud of you Grandson!

Dear Brother

Across the miles I send my love,
Even though we've been apart.
Memories of you I keep,
Tucked safe within my heart.

Time or distance does not change,
The love I have for you.
Many things I've wanted to say,
And hope you've loved me too.

We can't change what's in the past,
I surely wish I could.
Loved ones sometimes drift apart,
Don't stay together as we should.

I send these words so you will know,
I miss you my dear Brother.
I pray sincerely one day soon,
We may be with one another.

Fall Of Our Lives

When I look back across the years,
So many things I'd like to say.
In my heart are still the thoughts,
Of our happy wedding day.

A beautiful life with you I've had,
So many memories we have made.
Together we've spent a lifetime,
And faced it unafraid.

I could never have found another,
That to me would be so dear.
Your sweetness and your kindness,
Seems to grow with every year,

God gave me a special blessing,
When you came into my life.
And forevermore I'll thank Him,
That you chose me for your wife.

My Buddy (Loss Of A Pet)

Memories of you are planted,
Deep within my heart.
You're my forever kind of friend
Even though we are now apart.

Through many years and days,
You became to me so dear.
Always sensed my feelings,
For me were always here.

You touched me with your loyalty,
Between us a bond did grow.
Little did I ever know.
That I would miss you so.

I'll cherish all these memories,
Which to me are, oh so dear.
Whenever I am feeling lonely,
My Buddy, they'll bring you near.

Evelyn Mann

A Special Brother

When I reflect on joyous times,
My thoughts find a way to you.
Memories bring to me a smile,
Even though I miss you too.

I think of your bravery and valor,
In all things you did excel.
For others you did risk your life,
You served your country well.

A devoted son who was loved,
One who smiled with pain concealed.
Not wanting others to be distressed,
Feelings within were not revealed.

A caring Husband and Father,
And a wonderful Brother too.
When happy moments I recall,
I'll always think of you.

My Sister

You've always been so special,
To me throughout the years.
I know with me you'll always be,
Through laughter and through tears.

Whenever I have a problem,
You're the one to which I go.
The right path and direction,
You always seem to know.

If I am blue and feeling sad,
You know just what to do.
You make the dark clouds roll away,
And make the sun shine through.

I'm blessed to have you in my life,
And in my heart you'll always dwell.
Not only are you my sister,
But are my friend as well.

Evelyn Mann

I Remember You

Sometimes things just happen,
And we don't understand.
But I'll be right beside you,
I'll be your helping hand.

I remember the Dad you were,
And the one you'll be again.
With help from God above,
This battle we will win!

A son I do remember too,
You're still the love of my life.
Each day I spend in prayer for God,
To see us through this strife.

I see how hard each day you try,
And see how far you've come.
You've touched so many with efforts,
For pain to overcome.

I trust my faith that things will change,
And we'll thank God above,
For the Father and the Son.
He'll return to us with love.

Mom

I wonder if you'll ever know,
Just what you mean to me,
And all the many joys you've brought,
To all the family.

You taught me of our Father's love,
And how He cares for me.
Together we asked for guidance,
In things we could not see.

You told me how Christ lived and died,
For all humanity.
I gave my life to Him one day,
Like Him, I've tried to be.

You've always asked for so little,
And yet, given so much.
Each day there seems to be someone,
Whose life that you have touched.

I'm sending this so you may know,
Much love I feel for you,
I know that whether near or far,
That you do love me too.

Evelyn Mann

Single Mom

There's a very special person,
Who deserves a lot of praise.
It happens she's a "Single Mom",
With children left to raise.

There are words of hurry and obey!
When her family begins to stir.
Thoughts of anyone being late,
To her does not occur.

When all are fed and lunches made,
They are ready to start the day.
As each one she checks over,
Words of love she stops to say.

Out the door and off they go!
Each one in their own direction.
Mom whispers a fervent prayer,
"Father give them your protection."

At work she tries to do her job,
Her mind wanders through the day.
Thoughts fall upon those that she loves,
And she stops again to pray.

A Child's Prayer

I stood quietly as this precious one,
Began her nightly prayer.
A prayer so simple and sincere,
None other does compare.

"God bless Mommy and Daddy too,"
She whispered soft and sweet.
"God please bless all my family,
And thanks for what we eat."

She thanked Him for the moon and stars,
The flowers and the trees.
For the puppy dog that loves her,
A thank you just for me.

Prayed as if He was beside her,
Like talking to her Dad.
Told Him she was so sorry that,
If ever she was bad.

She told Him that she loved Him,
And then she said "goodnight."
I felt tears within my eyes as,
I kissed and held her tight.

Evelyn Mann

All Alone And Lonely

The years pass by so quickly,
And now I'm all alone.
I wait for notes and letters;
Wait by the telephone.

All that I have are memories,
When we were a family.
The days and weeks and months go by,
And you I long to see.

I hope wherever you are today,
That my love you will feel;
Know that I am missing you,
And my loneliness is real.

I pray you'll take a moment,
To think of me today.
You can be sure I'll think of you,
For you and yours will pray.

Come Sit With Me Daddy

Come sit beside me Daddy,
Spend some time with me.
There's much I'd like to tell you,
With you I need to be.

I wish that you were not so tired,
Each day that you come home.
You always say that you need rest,
And need to be alone.

Please come and sit with me Daddy,
I have so much to say.
I'd like to tell you important things,
That happened to me today.

A cute little puppy followed me home,
That Mom won't let me keep.
It's now upstairs under your bed,
And it's fast asleep.

I lost my lunch money on the bus,
And thought I would not eat.
When I went to my lunch room chair,
Two cookies were on my seat!

Evelyn Mann

I tried out for the soccer team,
I think I did real good!
The coach said for you to telephone him,
Just as soon as you could.

I made an A on a test today,
My drawing was put on the wall!
I knew the answer to a question,
When the teacher my name did call.

At school we played a game of fun.
We chose who we'd like to be.
I said I wanted to be just like you!
When the question came to me.

Oh Daddy you have fallen asleep!
You didn't hear what I've said.
Maybe tomorrow we can spend some time,
Before I'm put to bed.

I wish you could have given me,
A little hug and kiss.
I wanted to say that I love you,
And you I sure do miss.

Daughter-In-Law

You are someone who is special to me,
Have become more dear each day,
As I see your life before me,
There's so much I'd like to say.

You're always willing to lend a hand,
Are there when things go wrong.
You're just the perfect Daughter in Law,
I had waited for so long.

More like my daughter as days go by,
Who could ask for a better friend,
How thankful I am to be blessed,
By the one our Father did send.

As time goes by remember this,
In whatever you might do,
Just know my heart is full of love,
This day my dear for YOU!

Inspiration

Evelyn Mann

I Said A Prayer For You

I said a prayer for you today,
For you and those you love.
I prayed you'd feel God's presence,
Feel His guidance from above.

I asked Him to keep you safe and warm,
To send an angel before you.
To make a path and light the way,
In whatever you might do.

I have put you in His loving care,
I trust Him with all my heart.
He's faithful in His promises,
From you He will not part.

When tomorrow comes please tell me,
that you said a prayer for me.
Friends praying for each other,
Is what our Father loves to see.

God's Gift

God gave each of us a gift,
One we may never know.
Unless we learn to use that gift,
It may never show.

It may be something we can't hear,
Or something we can't see.
It's surely deep within us though,
Is what we need to be.

Let's seek out our special gifts,
And use them every day.
Try to make a difference,
Somewhere along the way.

If it happens you can't find it,
Just ask our Father above.
He's the one that gave the gift,
To you with all His love.

Evelyn Mann

Help Me Lord

Help me to show your love my Lord,
In everything I say and do.
Through me reflect your mercy and grace,
Let my light shine bright for you.

Help me to know how to serve you,
How to help those which you send.
Give me words to say to them,
That their broken hearts may mend.

Walk with me and guide me,
As I journey though the day.
I want to share my faith and love,
With those I meet along the way.

In all these things I'll praise your name,
And I'll give you the glory too.
Without you Lord there is no way,
I could do these things for you.

Legacy Of Dale Earnhardt

He treated me like family,
Although I was just a Fan.
My heart is heavy with sadness,
With the loss of this great man.

He was the master of the NASCAR!
Respected by all his peers.
He loved his friends and family,
It's for them I shed my tears.

I'll always remember in my heart,
Each time I go to the track.
That someone great is missing,
Who was always ahead of the pack.

The NASCAR fans will suffer loss,
This truth we all do know.
Dale is going to be missed by all,
To many he was their Hero.

Evelyn Mann

As I Remember

As I remember you my child,
I think of how I miss you.
I see your face before me,
In almost everything I do.

You gave me so much happiness,
A reason to face each day.
The years that we were all alone,
Love sustained us along the way.

One could not ask for a sweeter child,
Than the one God gave to me.
Even if just for a few short years,
On earth He let you be.

I won't forget the love we shared,
Your laughter and your smile.
Your love and kindness for all others,
Will be remembered all the while.

And now I will put my trust,
Into the hands of our Father above.
Knowing you were a part of His plan,
For His children that He loves.

Grandpa And Me

I came home from school one day,
And Grandpa was not there.
I searched all through the house,
Couldn't find him anywhere.

I went to his old rocking chair.
Wondering where he might be.
Someone touched my shoulder,
Sat me down upon their knee.

They said Grandpa had gone Home,
To be with our Father above.
That He had sent an angel,
To take him there with love.

I miss the walks and talks we had,
He told me of Jesus' birth.
We talked of God's creations.
In our wonderful world called earth.

I'm so glad he told me of our Lord,
How He lived and died for me.
I know when my life is ended,
My grandpa I will see!

Evelyn Mann

The Promise Of God

Sometimes trouble comes along,
And with it sadness and pain.
We may feel there's no way out.
There's nothing left to gain.

That's the time to renew our faith,
To listen to our Father's voice.
He wants to give us strength,
And help us make a choice.

Though things seem so hopeless,
No trial is too great.
God will give us comfort,
For us he does await.

As we go through the storms of life,
Just know He'll see us through.
God promised to never leave us,
He'll be watching over you.

While They Are Gone

While they are gone my Lord,
Protecting by land, sea and air.
Help us to not be afraid,
And not fall into despair.

We call upon your Holy name,
And claim your promises true.
To prepare the way for them,
As this mission they go through.

Walk with us while we wait,
Speak peace to our wounded hearts.
Let us feel your companionship,
Let your Spirit not depart.

You are the One who's in control;
We pray Thy will be done.
We'll give you the praise and glory
When the battle of war is won.

Evelyn Mann

Walk With Me

Today Lord, as we walk along,
Please guide the words I say.
Oh, lead me to that special one,
That I may help today.

I know there must be lonely souls,
That need a special friend.
Someone who asked in fervent prayer,
For someone you may send.

Give me the perfect words to say,
To tell them of your love.
A greater love they'll never know,
Than love that's from above.

Concern for them is in my heart,
I lift them up to you.
Oh, let them feel your precious love,
So they may know you too!

Please help me find the words to say,
To make them feel worthwhile,
And I will know that you and I,
Have helped them find their smile.

Without A Child

My Father, how she's truly prayed,
For children of her own.
She's kept her heart with you above,
And faithfulness she's shown.

She sees the children all around,
And how her heart does ache.
Sometimes she's so downhearted and,
She feels her heart will break.

The Bible says you have a plan,
And walk with us through life.
The scriptures never promised us,
That we'd be free of strife.

So Lord, please take her hand in yours,
To guide her as you may.
Help her to trust your perfect love.
And follow you each day.

And if she's not to have a child,
Please help her heart to see.
Help her to understand your plan,
Of what her life should be.

Evelyn Mann

Give Him The Day

There are days that come along,
That things just all go wrong.
It's not the day you planned to have,
One that seems so long.

We may walk in the midst of trouble,
Have a disappointing day.
No matter what we try to do,
Things get in the way.

Through it all we are not alone,
God watches from above.
He's there to rescue and will save,
And shower us with love.

He will quiet the troubled waters,
Make the wrong things right.
He will clear away the darkness,
So we may see the light.

He will handle all our problems,
If to Him we give the day.
He does not need our help when we,
Remember this and pray.

The Altar

As each came down to the altar,
With burdens they possessed.
They each asked for salvation and,
Their sins they had confessed.

I saw the tears fall down their face,
As on their knees they prayed.
Had come to the knowledge of Christ,
And the price He had paid.

I closed my eyes and felt tears come,
So full of love was I.
For Jesus Christ who loved me first,
So much that he did die.

I felt so very unworthy,
And said a silent prayer.
To praise and thank our God above,
That for me he could care.

Evelyn Mann

I prayed for those at the altar,
And asked God to bless.
To dry and wipe away their tears,
As their sins they did confess.

I know when days on earth are past,
A better place I'll be.
Because God gave His only son,
Who shed His blood for me.

An Invitation

He has prepared a place for us,
And sent invitations,
To more blessings than imagined;
Beyond expectations.

An angel stands beside the gate,
To welcome us all home.
And will lead us to our Father,
Who sits upon His throne.

There we will find a perfect peace,
And live in harmony.
With loved ones we will meet again,
And special friends we'll see.

It is filled with the warmth of love,
A place of joy and splendor.
The days of struggling and pain,
Are gone forevermore.

Thoughts of Heaven give us hope,
Of a life that's yet to be.
And God sends an invitation,
With love to you and me.

Evelyn Mann

Calvary

Implant in me a vision Lord,
Of how you died for me.
How you were crucified and bled,
That day on Calvary.

In that vision, oh let me see,
Thy sweet and tender mercy,
The everlasting love you have,
For someone such as me.

Help me to be worthy my Lord,
Of your love that is so great.
Let me feel your presence and,
Take time to meditate.

Keep me mindful of the cross,
When I am prone to stray.
Guide and direct me with thy hand,
In the things I do and say.

Oh how great is thy goodness!
I know one day I'll see.
Because you died on Calvary,
Forever with you I'll be!

Prayer Warrior

They are our Father's warriors,
An army armed with prayer.
You may call on them anytime,
Because they're always there.

Serving God in prayer for others,
With prayers that are sincere.
They pray with faith and do not doubt,
That God above does hear.

Prayer requests come from near and far,
From some they may not know.
Each one they hold close to their heart,
As prayers from them do flow.

Requests come from all walks of life,
None are too big or small,
This mighty army of our Lord,
Prays for one and all.

I thank my Father up above,
For those He calls to pray.
May He grant a special blessing,
Upon them every day.

Evelyn Mann

A New Day

Yesterday is now gone My Lord,
And promises were true.
You carried me with gentle wings;
Your love did help me through.

Please carry me through today Lord,
I need to know you're there,
Walk with me and talk with me.
So burdens I may share.

Guide my footsteps and I'll not fear,
What this day may hold.
With my hand in yours my Lord,
I can face what might unfold.

I won't worry about tomorrow,
Cause it's another day.
I'll claim again your promise true;
That You will show the way.

Fireflies

I amble down a mountain path,
While dusk is drawing near.
I need to see the lovely site,
I know will soon appear.

I've waited for this special time,
Excitement builds in me.
I hope to see those lights of God,
Because of love I'll see.

There in the midst of soft, still air,
While sweetly, twilight falls,
The sounds of night rise from the trees
My spirit, nature calls.

At last the sunlight disappears,
Then fireflies appear.
They glitter like the stars at night,
With lights so crystal clear.

Evelyn Mann

And then the magic does begin,
With thousands in accord.
Together with their magic lights,
They use that light they've stored.

The male has the brighter lamp,
The lady's light is weak.
Yet all their lights do synchronize,
To bring the courtships peak.

Yes, in this special place of God,
These courtships blend their light.
While proper mates are found for each,
I'm blessed to see this sight.

(Author's Note: This is a true happening near Elkmont State Park during a visit to Elkmont, Tennessee.)

Treasured Memories

Treasured memories of answered prayer,
Are tucked within my heart.
Days of tender mercies shown,
From me will never part.

We all have special memories when,
Hearts were full of despair.
We felt so all alone and thought,
There was no one to care.

Remembrance brings back the days,
God answered a special prayer.
Days we needed encouragement,
And our Lord was right there!

He answers prayers in many ways,
Some quite unexpected.
It may not be the way we prayed,
But God is protective.

So, I give thanks in remembrance of,
Previous answered prayer.
And strive to build new memories,
With others I may share.

Evelyn Mann

Hold On To Me

Should I wander from thee my Lord,
Please hold on to me.
Keep me on the righteous path,
The place where I should be.

Stay with me throughout the day,
So to your arms I may flee.
Whenever I feel temptation,
Let thou my example be.

Oh Lord, prompt me throughout the day,
Of things I should obey.
Show the right direction I should take,
If I am prone to stray.

Keep me mindful of your love and,
May I learn to love through you.
Then reflect your precious love in,
All things I may do.

May I forever keep the cross,
Close within my heart.
In remembrance may I seek you,
When each new day does start.

God Of Our Heart

God knows the number of the stars,
He calls them each by name.
He is the God of galaxies,
Such greatness we proclaim!

He spoke and the heavens were made,
His creations stand steadfast!
There's nothing in the Universe,
That could ever be surpassed!

He controls planets in their orbits,
There's nothing He can't do!
Yet, God in heaven still stoops down,
To care for me and you.

He knows our disappointments and,
How our hearts do ache.
He knows the pain and weeping,
On nights we lay awake.

Evelyn Mann

He will heal our broken hearts if,
We give Him each piece.
Then He will put them back for us,
And soon the pain will cease.

There is no limit to God's love,
He'll meet our every need.
If we will yield to His love,
Each footstep He will lead.

Looking Down

I've been looking down and waiting my child. . . to see if time was going to help you with your grief. Today as I look down, I feel there is something I need to say to you. I know you don't understand why I left you and Mom. There was a reason my child. Our Heavenly Father called me home. Whatever the reason He allowed me to stay with you if even for a little while; you must know that there was a reason.

Our Father has a plan for each of our lives, and no one knows how long He will allow us to be on earth. You must cherish each moment you spend there, learn everything you can about our Father . . . believe and trust in Him. Ask Him daily to show you YOUR purpose on earth. Study His Word and He will tell you.

I want you to dry up your tears now my dearest child.
I haven't stopped loving you and I will always be with
you in your heart. I need you to help take care of Mom
now for me . . . be brave for her.
If you but ask, our Heavenly Father will help you to be
strong. His loving arms will surround you and Mom
and help you to go forth in faith.

I'm depending on you my child. As I look down
tomorrow, I hope to see you smiling again . . . and will
you see if you can get Mom to smile for me too?

A Faithful Servant

We know our special friend,
You have loved with a giving heart,
There's things we want to say to you,
As now we come to part.

You've lived your life before us,
Reflecting our Father's love.
You've done your very best,
To give messages from above.

Your sweet and gentle spirit,
Is one we won't forget.
We've seen your love for Jesus,
From the day that we first met.

A good and faithful servant,
To our Father you have been.
We bow our heads and thank Him,
For the one that He did lend.

Evelyn Mann

If I Make A Wish

I've been told if I make a wish,
On a star that's shiny and bright,
That an angel will hear that spoken wish,
Sometime before its light.

The angels know the stars by name,
Our Father taught them that.
They know the one that's wished upon,
About them they do chat.

They take each wish as it's sent above,
Sort them out and put them in place.
Grant those first for someone in need,
For someone with tears on their face.

Don't give up on the wish you make,
If it's not granted right away.
Have faith that it's in an angel's care,
To our Father they will convey.

Always Here

Sometimes it's hard to understand,
Why things happen as they do.
Especially when you lose someone,
Who has been a friend to you.

We know not of tomorrow,
But one thing we can be sure.
God knows your grief and sorrow;
He will help you to endure.

You'll always have the memories,
Of someone who did care.
Will remember a special friendship,
And the times you two did share.

I'm always here if you need a friend.
Just know you can call on me.
I hope that when tomorrow comes,
A brighter day that you may see.

Evelyn Mann

How I Love Thee

How I do love Thee, oh my Lord.
I praise your Holy name.
From the first when I did know you,
My life's not been the same.

Each time I come to you in prayer,
I feel your love anew.
I seem to see my faults within,
Want more to be like you.

I pray that I may show my love,
That yours will show through me.
May words convey how great thou art,
That all around may see.

I give my life to you my Lord,
To do with what you may.
I will follow, love and serve you,
Glorify you every day.

I Bring This Child

Dear Heavenly Father . . .
I bring this child to you.
To help me love and nurture her,
The way you want me to.

Help me to make a commitment to self,
That regularly I will pray.
Scriptures help me each day to teach,
Lead this child to you one day.

A place of worship I will need,
An example I must be.
My Love for my Heavenly Father,
Each day this child must see.

Help me to find a quantity of time,
With her to spend each day.
So she may know I love her,
In a very special way.

Evelyn Mann

The Children Of God

We are all God's children,
He knows us each by name.
For it was He that made us,
There are no two the same.

He bestowed upon us privileges,
And gave us all a choice.
He sent to all a message,
To listen to His voice.

God has not left his children!
All our fears to Him are known.
We must have faith and trust Him,
As He sits upon His throne.

He's there when trouble rages!
With us in sadness and pain.
The cries we send in prayer,
Are not sent in vain.

Let's assure those around us,
Comfort and show them love.
Tell them He is with us!
Always in Spirit from above.

Mama Don't Go

It was the strangest dream I had,
I was sitting by Mama's bed,
And although our eyes did meet,
Not a single word was said.

In my heart I knew all the words,
That she wanted to say.
And felt she knew she wouldn't last,
Through another day.

I felt my heart was breaking,
As the tears ran down my face.
I'd never know the joy again,
Of her loving, sweet embrace.

Mama, please don't go away,
There's much I want to say.
In tears my heart cried out to her,
Stay with me another day.

Evelyn Mann

Heaven's portals opened up,
An angel led her inside.
As she turned and smiled at me,
I saw Jesus at her side.

These words I write to you in love,
For loved ones that may depart.
Don't leave those precious words unsaid,
That are are held within your heart.

Our Shepherd

What a privilege we have each day,
To go to Him in prayer.
A precious friend above all else,
And One who's always there.

Stronger than any obstacle,
That we could ever face.
Yet, like a gentle shepherd who,
Within His arms embrace.

He promised to never leave us,
By our side he will stay.
God always keeps His promises;
He's with us through each day.

When disappointments come our way,
And heartache we do feel,
Let's open up our hearts to Him,
And trust that He will heal.

As we travel down life's pathway,
Ask Him to go along.
Feel His sweet presence and the joy,
Of His love that's so strong.

Evelyn Mann

A Lonely Man

Out on the mission field of God,
There stands a lonely man.
One that preaches our Father's word,
To everyone he can.

He cares for all those around him,
Some haven't read God's word.
He's committed his life to tell them,
Of a Christ they haven't heard.

And yet this lonely man does long,
For one to love and share.
To help him in his ministry,
For those that need his care.

Though love for God does sustain him,
As he journeys through the day,
He prays that God will bless him with,
A helpmate along the way.

When you think of this lonely man,
Remember him in your prayers.
He's a precious child of our God,
One for whom He cares.

Create A New Heart

Create a new heart in me Lord,
So close to you I'll stay.
Give me strength to meet my trials,
When I am prone to stray.

With understanding guard my heart,
And each and every thought.
Keep me from things that displease you,
And do the things I ought.

Give me each day what you deem best,
Whether it's pain or pleasure.
I can make the day with your strength,
Your love beyond measure.

When day is gone and night is here,
And I do search my heart.
I want to know I've done my best,
From your will not to part.

You are the strength of my heart, Lord,
And so hard I will try.
That I may be worthy to serve you,
In my life your word apply.

Evelyn Mann

Looking Back

If ever we look back in time,
See bad things turned to good,
We have glimpsed our Father's mercy,
As promised that we would.

We can trace God's hand in our life,
And have the assurance,
That He transformed wrong things to right.
He gave us endurance.

As we face the uncertainties,
That each new day may bring,
God knows what we are facing and,
To His promise we can cling.

Our God gives us hope and mercy,
For us He is concerned.
These are the things He promised us,
For these we all do yearn.

We can choose to live above regrets.
Accept His joy and peace.
Know that He's watching over us,
His love will never cease.

Forever Kind Of Angel

When I look to the heavens above,
Somehow I feel you near.
I think of how much I love you,
And to me still so dear.

You were an angel sent to earth,
To fill our hearts with love,
A Forever Kind of Angel,
Sent from heaven above.

We didn't know you'd leave so soon,
That God for you would send.
An angel would hold you in His arms,
And heaven with you ascend.

Uncomplaining and courageous,
You smiled through all the tears.
So much faith and understanding,
For one so young in years.

Evelyn Mann

I'm thankful for the time we had,
For time we'll have again.
Together we will be once more,
But only God knows when.

Until I see you once again,
I'll hold you in my heart,
The sweet memories of my angel,
From me will never part.

Only Trust Him

We live our lives as best we can,
And things seem truly good.
Love and family all around,
All doing things we should.

And yet, somehow things do go wrong,
Tragedy comes our way.
We feel our life is over and,
Don't want to face each day.

Listen, and we can hear His voice!
He comes to give us hope.
God speaks words to our weary heart,
So with strife we may cope.

He knows the sadness in our life,
Is standing by our side.
He wants His light to shine through us,
With us He does abide.

Evelyn Mann

He will prepare the way for us,
As through the day we go.
Will help us find the greatest love,
That we can ever know.

He'll take the bad and make it good,
Only trust Him . . . you will see!
There will never be a moment,
That without Him we will be.

We are His precious children,
And for us He does care.
Just call upon His Holy name,
And know that He'll be there!

A Mother's Plea

Oh Father hear our prayers today,
For our children far away.
Please send your Angel Warriors,
To lead the path each day.

As our children march in battle,
Give them your direction;
Wrap your loving arms around them,
And give them protection.

I know that they must think of home,
And those they left behind.
Please let them feel our presence when,
Our thoughts may intertwine.

Let them know that we are with them;
Support them all the way.
We'll keep the home fires burning,
While they are gone away.

Evelyn Mann

They are the love of our life and,
So very proud are we!
To know they fight for others that,
One day they may be free.

We put them in your loving hands,
We know you're in control.
Please bring them home, dear Father,
And all our hearts console.

Dear Jesus

Jesus, hear my prayer tonight,
I need you really bad.
Mom and Dad are fighting again,
And it makes me really sad.

I hear them yelling all sorts of things,
And it scares me so.
I really don't know what to do,
There's no where I can go.

I love them both so very much,
Will you stop the yelling?
I've cried so many tears tonight,
How many there's no telling.

Please make this a happy home,
How glad I would be.
To have a happy family,
For Mom and Dad and me.

Evelyn Mann

Please answer this one prayer;
I'll try hard to be good.
I will come and talk everyday.
And love you like I should.

I know you can do this Jesus,
And pray with all my heart.
That when tomorrow comes,
The yelling will not start.

The One I See

I see a man with kindness,
Walking through a crowd.
Talking about our Father's love;
Eternal life he vowed.

The son of God and Messenger,
To all that were on earth.
Fulfilled what was prophesied,
By His manger birth.

Was sent to us with a mission,
That every one would hear.
That God loved each and everyone,
To Him each is so dear.

A lunch multiplied and all were fed;
People healed by his hand.
Some regained their sight again,
At our Lord's command.

Evelyn Mann

He taught them how they should live;
How to have eternal life.
Taught them to love their neighbor and,
Help them through their strife.

Because of this he suffered, so
That each of us might live.
On a cross at Mount Calvary,
His life He did give.

I thank you my sweet Jesus, and
When I stand before thee.
I pray I will be worthy of,
What you did for me.

A Day Will Come

How can we face another day,
When one we love is gone.
It's very hard to carry on,
And days just seem so long.

We hurt inside and tears we shed,
Because we miss them so.
Hard to reason and understand,
Why they had to go.

We think of them all through the day,
So hard for us to part;
Cry out for God to take the pain,
That overwhelms our heart.

God tells us that He is with us;
I know His word is true.
He speaks throughout His holy Word,
Sends hope to me and you.

Evelyn Mann

Accept His love and comfort and,
Give Him your aching heart.
He'll wrap his arms around you and,
From you He will not part!

Soon a day will come and,
You will smile once more.
As you recall the memories,
That last forevermore.

As We Walk

I turn my eyes to the heavens,
And know God hears my prayer.
I know He watches over me,
All day I feel Him there.

We walk together side by side,
And talk by waters still.
He reassures and comforts me,
My heart with love does fill.

Whenever my days are dark and drear,
I know that he is there.
When I fall He lifts me up and,
Is there with tender care.

My hand in His, I'm not afraid,
As I journey through the day.
I know that with His love and strength,
He will make a way.

Special Occasions

Evelyn Mann

Teacher

When I think of all the teachers,
That I have known each year.
You truly are remembered,
As the one I hold so dear.

You made me feel so special,
As each day you watched me grow.
I learned how to try my best,
When I did, you seemed to know.

Many students you have inspired,
To be the best that they can be.
Some are bound for leadership,
Their accomplishments you can see.

As now you take a different path,
Remember always in your heart.
Knowledge that you taught and shared,
From your students will not part.

My Pastor

We're so thankful to our Father,
To have a friend like you.
When we need an encouraging word,
You know just what to do.

You lift us up to our Father above,
Pray with tears that are so sincere.
Know the words that are in our heart,
Those that bring our Father near.

You sense our pain and suffering,
When a loved one we do lose.
Know words to give us comfort,
Words that He would choose.

If you need a friend to say a prayer,
Look around and you will see.
Friends that are ready and willing,
Because friends we'll always be.

Evelyn Mann

As You Graduate

May every treasured memory,
Bring happiness today.
Everyone of them remembered,
On your Graduation Day.

All the many dreams you had,
And shared along the way.
The many happy promises,
Will all come true this day.

You should be proud you've come so far,
And choices you have made.
Determination you held so fast,
Has helped you make the grade!

I send you Congratulations,
And wish you much success.
In all the things that you have done,
You gave your very best.

I'll keep you in my prayers this day,
And ask the Lord above,
To keep you always in His care,
And bless you with His love.

Birthday Wishes

You are like a ray of sunshine,
On days dark and drear.
A light that follows me around,
One that draws me near.

Someone that I can call upon,
To join with me and pray,
For my deepest needs and desires,
On any given day.

You share in my joys and sorrows,
A helping hand you'll lend.
Are ready at a moments call,
You are my best friend.

Always a smile upon your face,
So honest and sincere.
It is no wonder that to me,
You have become so dear.

You've made a difference in my life,
And on your special day,
I send my love and gratitude,
And wish you a happy Birthday!

Evelyn Mann

Wedding Wishes

Your wedding is a perfect time,
To ask our Lord above,
To keep you always in His care,
And bless you with His love.

I pray the home that you will share,
Has much joy and laughter,
And a special kind of love that,
Will last forever after.

May the sweet and precious moment,
When you pledge eternal love,
Be just the very beginning,
Of the life you've dreamed of.

I'm sending congratulations,
Especially for you,
And wish you many happy years,
As your dreams come true.

Our Anniversary

I used to dream of many things,
That I might want to be.
Dreamed with whom I'd spend my life,
Who God would choose for me.

I dreamed of places far away,
And the things I would see.
Dreamed about a special place,
One chosen just for me.

And now there is no need for dreams,
I dream not anymore.
For I did find the only one,
That I love and adore.

No need to travel to distant shores,
Or try to find my place.
Because I know that it is true,
It's found in your embrace.

You are the one I dreamed about,
In dreams so long ago.
And on our Anniversary,
I still do love you so.

Evelyn Mann

I Bring This Child (Baby Dedication)

Dear Heavenly Father.
I bring this child to you.
To help me love and nurture her,
The way you want me to.

Help me to make a commitment to self,
That regularly I will pray.
Scriptures help me each day to teach,
Lead this child to you one day.

A place of worship I will need,
An example I must be.
My Love for my Heavenly Father,
Each day this child must see.

Help me to find a quantity of time,
With her to spend each day.
So she may know I love her,
In a very special way.

Happy Birthday Daughter

Each day I know that I am blessed,
Whenever I think of you.
A special angel sent by God,
It shows in all you do.

I can share my joys and sorrows.
Know you're always there.
To have an understanding heart,
And show that you do care.

It's so nice to have a daughter,
That also is a friend.
Someone to laugh and talk with,
And with the day to spend.

My heart is full of love and pride,
For you my daughter dear.
And I wish you Happy Birthday!
With love that's so sincere.

I Pledge My Love

Outside of the realm of this world,
I take your hand in mine,
And as we soar above the clouds,
I feel a love sublime.

Here I promise my love to you,
Now and forever more.
A love beyond comprehension,
For one that I adore.

A love across time and measure,
One with comfort and peace.
Love that will travel the universe,
As I, my love release.

Closer together and more in love,
God heard my heartfelt cry.
I pledge my love to you this day,
And His Majesty Most High.

Happy Anniversary

I felt all alone and lonely,
And then God sent me you.
I had prayed for you all my life;
Love that was sweet and true.

I knew the day that I met you,
That you would be the One.
My love for you began to grow,
As each new day begun.

I love the sweetness and kindness,
Each day that's shown to me;
The understanding love you give,
To all my family.

You are all I've ever wanted,
And oh! so much more.
A love I'd always dreamed about,
But never known before.

Evelyn Mann

So many things I want to say,
On our anniversary.
Words are deep within my heart that,
I hope that you may see.

You've filled my life with happiness,
That is beyond compare.
I cherish each and every day,
That together we share.
Happy Anniversary . . . I love you!

Thank You

When burdens are heavy to carry,
You stretch out a hand.
When I feel that I can't make it,
You show me that I can.

In everything you stand by me,
When others turn away.
And all the things you've done for me,
In my heart will stay.

If in this world, there were no you,
It would be so drear.
The friendship that you offer is,
So honest and sincere.

I know that I am better and,
I know I'm blessed by you.
I send these words of "Thank You,"
For all the things you do.

Holidays

Evelyn Mann

Times Remembered

Many memories come to mind,
With the ending of the year.
As I recall days gone past,
Some even bring a tear.

We have had a shattered dream,
Had problems to come our way,
Many have felt we were alone,
Afraid to face another day.

Through it all we had a friend,
That was with us all the way!
One that stood beside us,
And heard when we did pray.

When we dream our dreams anew,
In the New Year we will start.
Let's all invite our Father,
In our dreams to have a part.

Loving Thoughts Of Mom

I don't think you really know,
Just what you mean to me.
The sweet and precious love you give,
To our whole family.

Patient and understanding,
In each and every way.
I know that I do love you more,
With every passing day.

I send this Valentine to you,
To remind you of my love.
For you I am so thankful,
To our Father up above.

Evelyn Mann

To My Valentine

You'll always be my Valentine,
As you have all through the years.
Together we have always shared,
Days of happiness and tears.

You could not offer more,
Than the love that you do give.
Precious love so sweet and true,
I'll cherish as long as I live.

You try to make each day for me,
As beautiful as can be.
Everyday my heart is filled,
With the love I hope you see.

There will never be another you,
So I keep you in my heart.
Hope you know my love for you,
From me will never part.

My Valentine

You are my special Valentine,
The one I hold so dear.
My love for you just seems to grow,
Ever stronger through each year.

I am so thankful for the love,
That you so freely give.
I shall thank our Father above,
As long as I may live.

Stay with me my Valentine,
Just let me feel your love.
Let me feel your sweetness,
That is kin to that above.

When this time is long, gone past,
In all things that I may do.
I will know that I was blessed,
My Valentine by you.

Evelyn Mann

Will You Be My Valentine?

How can I help but love you,
With your funny little ways.
You've brought joy to my heart,
Oh! so many days.

In all this world, of those I know,
You are the most sincere.
The way you make me smile and laugh,
Has made you very dear.

There's a special way about you,
That's loving and so sweet.
You touch my heart in many ways,
Every time we meet.

There's something I've wanted to ask,
For a very long time.
I hope you know it's from my heart,
Will you be my valentine?

My Valentine To You

I think of how I could not see,
The answer to my prayer.
One I had prayed for all my life.
Has always been right there.

I spent endless nights wondering,
Who God would send to me.
Sometimes those that are close to us,
Are blessings we can't see.

You've stood by me in good and bad,
In happy days and sad.
You've been the very dearest friend,
That I have ever had.

I send this Valentine to you,
With you I want to be.
And say a thankful prayer to God,
For what you've meant to me.

Evelyn Mann

My Puppy Valentine

You're always there to greet me,
Each and every day.
Happy with just a little pat,
Nothing I need to say.

Looking at me with big brown eyes,
Just melts my heart in two.
Little long ears all laid back,
Nothing as sweet as you.

We've traveled a hard road this year,
God blessed in many ways.
He put his loving hand on you,
As I asked so many days.

We have a lot to look forward to,
You can run and romp and play!
God is so faithful to answer,
Prayers for pets we pray,

You are still the sweetest puppy dog,
That I have ever had.
You are my puppy valentine,
Even when you're bad!

Would You, Could You?

My heart just goes pitter patter,
When you are around.
I see your sweet smile and then,
My heart begins to pound!

You could charm the birds from the trees,
With your sweet little way.
No wonder that I love you more,
And do each passing day.

You make such a difference in my life,
Make it come together.
I know with you close by that I,
Can keep it altogether.

Such a sweet and precious heart,
That I would love for mine.
Would you, could you, let me,
Be your valentine?

Evelyn Mann

Be Mine

I'd love to look into your eyes,
And be with you today.
You fill my heart with many things,
That I would like to say.

I love the way you smile and laugh,
With that funny little way.
Just makes me want to hug you,
Though so far away.

My love this day I send to you,
And hope you know it's true.
There's no one else I care about,
The way I care for you.

I want to say I love you;
Won't you please be mine?
You'll make me oh! so happy if,
You'll be my valentine!

My Heart Belongs To Only You

You've become part of my life,
I think of you all day long.
My heart never knew it could feel,
A love that is so strong.

My thoughts are of you at night time,
In my dreams I see you.
I love to feel your presence there,
And feel your sweet love too.

Oh, I wish my dreams could come true,
Of that dreamland place.
No sweeter time that I could know,
Than to gaze upon your face.

I'll keep you close within my heart,
Filled with love so true.
I send these words so you will know;
My heart belongs to only you.

Easter Greetings

Oh! what a beautiful morning!
I've just dropped in to say.
I hope you have a beautiful,
And wonderful Easter Day.

Flowers are blooming everywhere,
Bird songs are in the air.
Spring is unfolding her treasures,
And wants us all to share.

Easter gives hope for tomorrow,
As after the winter comes Spring.
Our hearts can be filled with gladness,
As hearts rejoice and sing.
Happy Easter!

Easter Joy

A pretty dress to match her eyes,
Much like an azure blue.
Lacy socks and new white shoes and,
An Easter bonnet too!

All dressed up and feeling pretty;
Easter basket held so tight.
She looked like a little angel,
That comes in Easter's light.

Her Daddy led the way with his,
Sweet and loving touch.
Helped her look for Easter eggs that,
She'd looked forward to so much!

She smiled and laughed with glee as,
Treasures were uncovered.
Peeping from underneath a leaf,
Waiting to be discovered.

Evelyn Mann

No doubt that this is Daddy's girl!
I see it in his eyes.
She is his love, his joy, his life,
One he does idolize.

I watched as they made memories,
Those that would be so dear.
A basket filled with candy eggs,
That soon would disappear!

I am so filled with Easter Joy;
And all the love it brings.
Because my Lord does live today,
My heart forever sings!

He Is Risen

I sing praises to my Lord!
For what He did for me.
He took my sins upon Himself,
And died at Calvary.

My Lord lay in a cold, dark tomb,
A stone placed at the door.
Tears were shed and cries were heard,
From ones that did adore.

What a joyous time was to come,
The stone was rolled away.
My Lord Jesus arose from the grave!
Forever will he stay.

When my journey on earth is done,
And see His glorious face,
I will spend my days of eternity,
In that Heavenly place.

This gives hope of what's to come and,
Reason to serve Him too.
Let's all join our hearts in praise for;
What He did for me and you.

Evelyn Mann

A Risen Savior

I worship a risen Savior,
Who's all the world to me.
He gave His life that I may live,
One day on Calvary.

He is my comfort and my strength,
A friend that's always there.
When trouble comes or fears arise,
I know I'm in His care.

His sweet love is like no other,
That I have ever known.
He's faithful in His promises;
I know I'm not alone.

Today He sits upon His throne,
One day I know I'll see.
Because He died on Calvary,
And love He has for me.

A Rose For Mom

May I give my Mom a Rose,
To let her know I'm here?
I always did when on earth;
I know she'll feel me near.

I'm sure that she will think of me,
On this her Mother's Day.
I was her beloved child,
But I had to go away.

I hope she knows I love her,
And will for eternity.
Father says that some day,
She'll be here with me.

When she sees this rose so sweet.
She'll know I've found a way.
To send her hugs and kisses,
And a rose for Mother's Day.

Evelyn Mann

Mom

I want to say I love you,
In a very special way.
You mean so very much to me,
You're in my thoughts each day.

I love the time I spend with you,
And the laughter that we share.
The special times when we talk,
I know you really care.

I know that I can count on you,
If ever I need a friend.
And if I'm feeling a little sad,
Your shoulder you will lend.

As Mother's Day comes around,
I hope you feel my love.
I pray our Father sends you,
A special blessing from above.

Happy Mother's Day Grandmother

You are so special in my life,
I'm blessed because of you.
For the love that you have given,
Has always seen me through.

Many memories we have shared,
Of special times and days.
You always make them beautiful,
With your sweet thoughtful ways.

May the good you've done for others,
Return to you this day,
And know that you are loved by all,
In a very special way.

I pray for you much happiness,
And joy in every way.
My love I send and wish for you,
A Happy Mother's Day!

Evelyn Mann

Special Mom

God sent me a special Mom,
One He selected with much care.
He knew I had a special need.
You were the answer to my prayer.

There are so many memories,
That together we have shared.
I'm so glad we've had each other,
And to know each other cared.

I know that we shall always have,
This special bond of love.
Because it is a gift from God,
Sent to us from above.

I send my love on Mother's Day,
With this message so sincere.
Because you are my Special Mom,
The one I hold so dear.

Happy Father's Day

I may not always show it,
In the things I say and do,
But there are many things,
I feel inside for you.

I thank you for the little things,
That's meant so much to me.
Things that come so natural,
You hardly ever see.

You've never been too busy,
To talk to me a while.
You're always glad to see me,
And greet me with a smile.

Through the years you taught me,
To always do what's right.
For all the things remembered,
I give thanks for every night.

Evelyn Mann

And so I send these words to you,
In hopes that you will see.
Especially on this Father's Day,
How much you mean to me!
I love you Dad.

Happy Thanksgiving

Together let us join our hands,
On this Thanksgiving Day.
Let us join our hearts as well,
As we bow our heads to pray.

Give thanks for friends and family,
For food that He has supplied.
All the wondrous things He's done,
And the needs He does provide.

If we hear of someone lonely,
Let's ask them our food to share.
Tell them about our Father's love,
And show them that we care.

I'll be thinking of YOU! this day,
Of Thanksgiving days gone past.
The memories of your friendship,
In my heart will forever last.

Evelyn Mann

Give Thanks

Autumn leaves are falling,
Pretty colors everywhere.
Thanksgiving Day is almost here,
Another day that we may share.

The things we take for granted,
Are blessings from above.
The needs He has provided,
Were given to us in love.

Let's give thanks for what we have,
Bow our heads and together pray.
As we join our friends and family,
On this Thanksgiving Day.

Thanksgiving Blessings

Oh Lord as we give thanks this day,
For blessings you bestow.
Help us to have compassion for,
Those we may not know.

Help us to reflect your sweet love,
In all that we might do.
So every life that we may touch,
Will feel your Presence too.

You have blessed us in many ways.
Some ways that may not show,
The days of joy and happiness,
Are those that we may know.

Each blessing is a special gift.
Let's take time to say today,
A prayer of thankfulness to God,
For blessings sent each day.

Evelyn Mann

The sweetest blessing we could have.
May be carried in our heart,
The assurance of God's sweet love,
From us he'll never part.

So, I thank you Lord for all you do,
And for your love sublime.
A very special kind of love,
That I may claim as mine.
I love you my Lord . . .

Christmas With You

All that I want for Christmas,
Is to spend the day with you.
A day of fun and laughter,
With some time for sharing too.

Time to remember baby Jesus,
As we look at a starry sky.
Think of how He lived on earth,
How He died for you and I.

Christmas carols playing softly,
A perfect Christmas tree.
Lots of lights and Christmas balls,
For everyone to see.

I put this wish first on my list,
And hope that it comes true.
Nothing could make me as happy,
Than to spend the day with you.

If my wish is not to be,
All my love I'll send to you.
Wish for you much happiness,
And a Merry Christmas Too!

Evelyn Mann

Christmas With Jesus

We know that you are happy now,
And we have to let you go.
Although it will not be easy,
A cheerful smile we'll show.

Christmas just won't be the same,
Because you are not here.
Yet I just seem to know somehow,
That we will feel you near.

We wonder how it is with you,
Spending Christmas up above.
Listening to the celestial choir,
Singing carols that we love.

You know we will always love you,
Especially on Christmas Day.
Something will always remind us,
Of your sweet and loving way.

One thing that we do ask of you,
You'll know just what to say.
We'd like to send a message,
And wish Jesus Happy Birthday!

A Christmas Kiss

Though it's been many years gone by,
It's still so clear to me.
My Mother held me in her arms,
As we sat near the tree.

She was feeling sentimental;
Told of Christmas' gone by.
She led me to the window and,
We looked up at the sky.

The night was bright and beautiful!
Bright stars everywhere.
With no beginning and no end,
To all the wonders there.

One star seemed to move from the rest,
And as we watched it fell.
Everything was so quiet and still,
It was like a magic spell!

Evelyn Mann

I saw a smile upon her face,
And tears formed in her eyes.
At the moment the star began,
To fall from darkened skies.

"That was a kiss from Grandma" she said,
"Who's in heaven above.
She sends a kiss each Christmas night,
To remind me of her love."

I think of Mom on Christmas night,
A star I wait to see.
As I know she's looking down and,
Will send a kiss to me!

The Birthday Story

Loaded down with her baby dolls,
To Grandma's house she came.
A hug, a kiss, a quick hello,
Smiled as she said my name.

As she stepped inside the door,
Things did not seem the same.
Her little face lit up with glee,
As her footsteps took their aim!

Straight to the Christmas tree she ran,
Sat down upon the floor.
Looking at the Christmas lights and,
Decorations galore!

I saw the wonder in her eyes,
And my heart she did touch.
When she saw the little statues,
The ones I love so much.

Evelyn Mann

She reached for Baby Jesus and,
Then held Him to her heart.
So began the Birthday story,
Told from the very start.
Happy Birthday Jesus!

The Greatest Gift

Christmas is coming very soon,
A time for joy and mirth.
Time to celebrate once again,
Our Savior Jesus' birth!

Most are truly happy to see,
Holidays come once more.
Decorations pretty and bright,
Christmas wreaths on the door!

Yet, there are some that feel lonely,
Family visits may be few.
Everyone is busy it seems,
So many things to do.

They wait and think of Christmas' past,
Oh! how sweet they were.
Santa Clause and Christmas trees!
The household all astir!

Evelyn Mann

They long to see their loved ones,
And hope it will be soon.
They think of happy times gone past,
When they hear a Christmas tune.

Maybe tomorrow they will come,
Dear Lord, please bring them home.
Oh, this would be the greatest gift,
That they have ever known!

Christmas Remembered

I think of Christmas' gone past,
So many years ago.
How I waited for Santa Clause,
The time would pass so slow!

I remember as a little girl,
Upon an old tire sled.
Sliding down a long, steep hill,
With little hands so red.

No scarf, no gloves, holes in my shoes;
But I didn't mind.
The chilling cold went unnoticed as,
I wore a coat well lined.

Christmas was very simple for,
The child and the mother.
Gifts under the tree were always sparse,
But we had each other.

Evelyn Mann

I remember once when Santa came.
He made my wish come true.
A beautiful doll with yellow hair,
And she had pigtails too!

Funny, the things that we remember,
Of days so long ago.
Cherished memories of Christmas times,
And playing in the snow,

Today I have new memories,
To keep within my heart.
Sweet family and friends so dear,
These will never part.

But I'll always remember that little girl,
Especially on Christmas Eve.
And the mother's sacrifice for,
The doll that I received.

Quiet Night

I sit here by my Christmas tree,
Enjoying visions I see.
Thoughts of Christmas' long gone past,
Cause mixed emotions for me.

I see ornaments with special meanings,
Those given by a friend.
Many things made by little hands,
Oh! what memories they lend.

I think of loved ones in the past,
And how things used to be.
So precious were those happy days,
When Christmas spent with me.

The soft glow of twinkling lights,
The quietness of the night.
Makes me think of Jesus birth;
And the Star that shined so bright.

Evelyn Mann

I also think of you tonight and,
Give thanks for you above.
I hope that you may feel my thoughts,
But most of all my love.

Together we two will not be,
But, if we were I'd say,
"I wish for you much love and joy,
Especially on Christmas Day!"

My Gift To You

I have a present just for you,
It's wrapped so carefully.
Although it doesn't have a card,
You'll know it is from me.

I hope that you will cherish it,
It's the most special thing I had.
To think it's all that I can give,
Makes me feel a little sad.

On Christmas morn I'll think of you,
With the gifts around your tree.
When there is one to open last,
Let that be the one from me.

Merry Christmas to you darling,
Even though we're miles apart.
I send this gift with all my love;
I give to you my heart.

Contact Evelyn Mann
www.reflectionsofsouthbreeze.com
or order more copies of this book at

TATE PUBLISHING, LLC

127 East Trade Center Terrace
Mustang, Oklahoma 73064

(888) 361 - 9473

Tate Publishing, LLC

www.tatepublishing.com